Inside the Family:
Changing roles of men and women

Occasional paper number 6

1987

Family Policy Studies Centre

The Authors

Melanie Henwood is a Research Officer at the Family Policy Studies Centre, and was formerly engaged in research at the University of Bath. Her main interests are in the areas of community care; child support; and housing policy in relation to the family life cycle. She is the co-author (with Malcolm Wicks) of *Forgotten Army: family care and elderly people* (1984), and *Benefit or burden? the objectives and impact of child support* (1986). She is editor of the *Family Policy Bulletin* which is published three times a year.

Lesley Rimmer was Deputy Director of the FPSC since its establishment in 1983, and has now left the Centre. She was previously a Research Officer with the Study Commission on the Family. She has worked on the staff of the House of Commons Treasury Select Committee and was also a senior lecturer in Economics at the South Bank Polytechnic. She is the author (or joint author) of a number of Study Commission papers, and of an FPSC briefing paper, *Divorce: the 1983 Matrimonial and Family Proceedings Bill* (1983). Her main interests are in community care; marriage; divorce and one parent families; and employment trends.

Malcolm Wicks is the Director of the FPSC and was the Research Director and Secretary to the Centre's predecessor — the Study Commission on the Family. He was formerly a lecturer at Brunel University, and a member of the Home Office Urban Deprivation Unit. He has also taught at York University and the Civil Service College, and was on the research staff at the Centre for Environmental Studies. His publications include: *Old and Cold: hypothermia and social policy* (1978) and *Government and Urban Poverty: inside the policy making process* (1983) (co-author). His most recent publication is *A Future for All: Do we need a welfare state?* (1987). He has also written a number of Study Commission and FPSC reports, articles and chapters.

Acknowledgements

We would like to thank all those who assisted in the preparation of this paper. Our Governing Council commented on an earlier draft, as did colleagues attending a staff seminar at the University of Kent, where a presentation was given. Lynne Gundy and Helen Robson prepared the final typescript for publication. Our thanks also to Spencer Rowell for the use of the cover photograph.

Contents:

Introduction Melanie Henwood

Section 1
The Family and the Home Melanie Henwood

Section Two
Family Care Melanie Henwood

Section Three
Paid Work Lesley Rimmer

Section Four
Income and Resources Lesley Rimmer

Summary Melanie Henwood

Section Five
Private Families and Public Policy
Malcolm Wicks

Although sections are by individual authors, this paper has been a collaborative exercise. Melanie Henwood acted as Editor and also in particular contributed parts of Section Four.

Introduction
Melanie Henwood

The Family In Crisis?

The family has long been the subject of sociological interest and controversy, and since the 1960s especially has come more and more to centre stage of public debate. The rhetoric surrounding the family is prolific, and the interpretations of what is happening to it are as varied as they are many. There are those, for example, who view the institution of 'The Family' as being in a state of crisis. They may point to such trends as a rising divorce rate; the disappearance of the so-called 'traditional' extended family, and the fragmentation of households, as signalling the death knell of the family. And indeed such a pessimistic view is nothing new.

A deep seated anxiety attaches to what Fletcher has termed this "universal concern about the family in society, and about those qualities of personal life and personal relationships which are so intimately bound up with it".[1] All generations probably find evidence of moral decline and social instability, as Knowles has observed:

"Englishmen are always despondent about their own times and it would be easy to quote contemporaries in every period so that their testimony would show that we had gone downhill ever since the time of the Norman conquest." [2]

Other pundits may argue to the contrary: that far from being a threatened species needing protection, the family as an institution remains deeply entrenched and forms a lynchpin in society as much today as it ever did.

The recent past has seen a surge of interest from the media in such topics. A nostalgia for past decades has been paralleled by an introspective obsession with 'the way we are today'. The Harris survey 'Britons Observed'[3] (conducted for The Observer in 1984); the birth of the annual British Social Attitudes Survey[4] in the same year; the London Weekend discussion programme 'Twenty Years On' in 1985; and the 1986 BBC2 series 'Lovelaw' which looked at love and marriage around the world, are just a few recent examples.

Politics and the Family

Political interest in the family has also been increasingly apparent. In recent years the welfare state has been seen by some (especially those associated with the New Right) as the particular enemy of the family and its traditional values.

Those who would promote these so-called 'Victorian values' of a strong work ethic; self-reliance; resourcefulness; endurance; self-respect and patriotism, fear what they see as the undermining effects of State intervention in realms of individual and family responsibility.[5]

"We are the Party of the family" declared Mrs Thatcher in 1977. Yet it is obvious that the family cannot be the *sole* province of the Right. No political party has a monopoly on the family, and interest is evident on all sides. The facts of political life ensure that any serious party will present itself as 'the party of the family' — albeit that this will assume quite different forms.[6]

Political interest in the family has been particularly marked since the late 1970s. James Callaghan, while Prime Minister, lamented the absence of a family focus in policy making. Patrick Jenkin, when Secretary of State for Social Services argued that "the central role of the family" needed to be reasserted in the social services. The work of the Ministerial Family Policy Group similarly stirred further interest (and some ridicule) just prior to the 1983 General Election. Leaked press reports revealed plans to encourage families to reassume responsibilities taken on by the State. And this proved highly sensitive. More recent examples of continued political interest in the family include recurrent disquiet over law and order; Norman Tebbit's condemnation of the legacy of a valueless 'permissive society'; concerns to include a moral element in sex education in schools; Neil Kinnock's admission of a "reactionary" stance towards his children's upbringing, and David Owen's observation that "Rights and responsibilities come together more in relation to family policy than in any other area of policy."[7]

The politicising of the family, and the emergence of pro-family, moral majority style organisations, may also be seen in the context of a number of other political developments: from the birth of 'youth culture' in the 1960s, and — perhaps more significantly — parallel with the rise of feminism and the women's movement, which have often been viewed as the antithesis of the family.

"Defenders of the family often locate feminists among those who criticize and would even destroy the family; the conservative 'pro-family' movement is explicitly anti-feminist. Critical analyses of the family, and efforts to change traditional family arrangements have been central to the women's movement (. . . .) Of all the issues raised by feminists, those that bear on the family (. . . .) have been the most controversial.[8]

Certainly feminism has criticised the ideology of 'the family' which views the traditional family and roles as the only legitimate or 'natural' form.

The Family Today

To ask 'what is happening to the family today?' is to enter into an area of some complexity in which there will inevitably be more questions than answers. The structural changes affecting the family may be fairly easily described and analysed: trends in household formation; patterns of marriage and divorce; the re-constitution of families; increased longevity and parallel changes in inter-generational relationships; changing experiences of employment and unemployment (and how these differ for men and women).

Such data present a sketch of the family as it is today. However, this is very much a description of the bare *structure* of the family unit. The ethnography which adds the colour and dimension to this account needs also to be painted in if our understanding is to have any depth and 'the family' is to have any qualitative substance.

Are the areas of structural change today being matched by changes in roles and relationships? This leads us to consider not only the quantitative data of trends, but also the area of attitudes, of values and beliefs. What can we say — for example — about gender, or about the sexual division of labour both inside and outside of the home? What, in short are the *dynamics* of the family today?

The stereotype of the family which is epitomised by the husband as the sole wage earner, wife as full time housekeeper and mother with dependent children living at home (that is, the family which is featured almost exclusively in the advertising world), in fact comprises only a *minority* of households at any given point in time.

However, this refers to a snapshot of the family. A useful distinction may be made between households and individuals. On the one hand, the diversity of family types may be seen in the fact that only 37% of households consist of a married couple with dependent (29%) or independent (8%) children.[9] Similarly, a breadwinning husband with a non-working wife at home with two dependent children accounts for a mere 8% of all working men.

If *persons* rather than households are considered, some 59% of people live in households headed by a married couple (with dependent or independent children). Another 20% of people comprise a married couple (most of whom have either had or will have children). Almost 80% of people then live in households headed by a married couple. The households and individuals distinction also illustrates the value of a life-cycle approach alongside a snapshot of the family; most people will pass through all or many of these stages in the course of a lifetime.

While it is true that 'the family' actually refers to a great many types — from the single parent to the three or four generational extended unit — the focus of this paper is *largely* upon the conventional family comprising adults and dependent children. We are not concerned here with the nature and substance of interaction between family members merely for its intrinsic interest, but for what it reveals about roles and role expectations.

Most people (nine out of ten) get married at some time in their lives; and nine out of ten of these married couples will have children. Even if one third of those marriages will end in divorce, it remains true that most people will spend the greater part of their lives growing up in, and subsequently forming, such families. Overall it is estimated that men spend 89% of their lives in a family, and women 82% (the differential reflecting women's greater life expectancy and higher probability of widowhood).[10] Some may go on to form different types of household at different stages in their life, but life within the nuclear family will be the most common experience. It is important therefore to know what this family today is like.

The Symmetrical Family?

The concept of the 'symmetrical family' developed by Young and Willmott[11] provides a further perspective on the family. They described a three-fold historical typology ranging from the pre-industrial stage, to the wage earning of industrialisation, and onto a third stage which they argued is still evolving.

This typology ascribes different characteristics to the family in each phase. In the first, pre-industrial, stage it is argued, the family was typically the unit of production: "for the most part, men, women and children worked together in home and field." This was depicted as something of a 'Golden Age' (which many historians would disagree with). In contrast, the second stage of industrial differentiation and specialisation struck at this family economy and introduced a hitherto unknown distinction between the worlds of work and 'life'. In the third (current) stage it is claimed that "the unity of the family has been restored around its functions as the unit not of production but of consumption"

"The new kind of family has three main characteristics which differentiate it from the sort which prevailed in Stage 2. The first is that the couple and their children are very much centred on the home, especially when the children are young . . ." [12]

This 'home centredness' is argued to produce a greater intimacy and privatising of family life: the nuclear family becomes of greater significance than the extended one, and — most significantly — it is claimed:

"(. . .) inside the family of marriage the roles of the sexes have become less segregated." [13]

This formed the basis of the concept of the *'symmetrical family'*. This is not to say that the roles of the sexes are identical, but Young and Willmott have argued:

"In this context the essence of a symmetrical relationship is that it is opposite but similar (. . . .) a term is needed which can describe the majority of families in which there is some role segregation along with a greater degree of equality than at Stage 2." [14]

New Man: An emerging species?

Whether or not it is to be seen as part of the evolution of the symmetrical family, certainly the 'new family' has been identified by some, and the focus has been very much upon the changed relations between men and women within marriage and other long term relationships. The sociological interest which focused on sexual politics through the rise of the women's movement is turning increasingly to examine the male role.

The label 'New Man' has been coined — at least in the pages of certain journals and newspapers. 'New Man', the fashion writers tell us, is recognisable by his style, but more broadly he is characterised by his rebuttal of the traditional images and pursuits of 'macho man'. Thus, 'New Man' is caring and demonstrative, slightly narcissistic, liberated and very laid back.

In part this identifying of a new species may be seen as an aspect of the current quasi-sociological trend which is eager to classify real or imagined social groups and cliques. This practice, epitomised by the identification of 'Sloane Rangers' in the late 1970s, has ploughed relentlessly through a catalogue of Yuppies, Yaps, Hooray Henries, Preppies, Droppies, Dinkies and Young Fogies, each with their own notorious exponents. 'New Man' is a prize exhibit in this hall of fame.

Analysis of the new species has been loose. Indeed it has been observed elsewhere that rhetorical exchange on the subject has far outpaced serious analysis.[15] The diverse features which have been identified are nonetheless viewed in some quarters as pointing towards an overall trend. A redefinition of 'masculinity' is seen by some as the inevitable response to the women's movement, and to other major social and cultural trends:

"One trend is that partnerships are being constructed to contain two separate as well as one joint identity, another is that the desire of more women to have careers will make it easier for their men to accept homecentred roles. A third trend is that men are having more time to think about their lives anyway, in the spaces between marriage and remarriage, which is an increasing social pattern." [16]

In addition to the legacy of the women's movement which has arguably forced some men to reconsider their roles in relation to the changes evident in partners, other factors may be relevant. The rise in unemployment will have introduced the new experience for some couples of women as the major breadwinner, and this may similarly have challenged traditional gender assumptions. The European attitudes survey conducted in 1983 found attitudes becoming more flexible — particularly among the young and highly educated, and attributed change in part to the chillier economic climate:

"Age and education, throughout the survey, usually turned out to be more important than sex in predicting people's attitudes. For instance, the traditional model of the family — where the man works and the woman runs the home — is now only seen as the ideal by fewer than three in ten Europeans. About four in ten of the over 50s still see it as the best division of roles, but only two in ten of the under 24s." [17]

Whether or not 'New Man' actually exists is perhaps not the concern of these pages. However, this does raise the question of changing roles and attitudes which *are* a central interest. Where an analysis of such change should begin is unclear; the worlds of home and work are intertwined.

Inside the Family

The Family Policy Studies Centre is especially concerned with understanding and describing contemporary family patterns, the changes that are taking place and the implications of such changes for policy and practice. This paper attempts to dig deeper than some of our previous work, to look beyond the trends and consider their impact (if any) in a more qualitative sense on the nature of family life and the roles of men and women as partners and parents.

In the following chapters we consider the organisation of household and domestic tasks; of child care (and of the care of dependants more generally); of paid work, and of the management of income and resources. The inter-relations of these are also explored. For example, we examine the interaction of paid and unpaid work, and in particular the relationship between the domestic division of labour and women's labour market participation.

The policy implications of some of these areas are also addressed. Is policy responding sufficiently to changing circumstances, or are policies — for example in the area of day care for young children — artificially constraining the options for many families? Moreover, what part do values play, and is the *internal* world of the family a legitimate area for public policy intervention?

To attempt to look "inside the family" potentially opens a Pandora's box. We could, for example, consider the inter-personal and psychological dimensions which make the family tick (or indeed tear it assunder). Instead we are concerned specifically with evidence of internal adjustments to traditional roles which *might* be expected given changing social circumstances. Whether any such change is desirable is a separate issue, and not one which we address. In the sections which follow we examine some aspects of the family in which change — or moves towards greater 'symmetry' — might be expected. Is the family today significantly different from, and more egalitarian than, that of previous decades and generations in such areas as the division of labour; the management and control of resources; employment, and care of dependent members?

Many of these areas clearly overlap and inter-relate: the pattern of employment outside of the home might be expected to influence the division of labour within the domestic sphere, and the control of resources. Does more or less equality or change in any one area herald more or less in others?

Moreover, if significant change *is* taking place, what might the broader implications be? For example, how appropriate are the assumptions about the family which underpin employment policy; national insurance and income tax regulations, and indeed, much of the fabric of the welfare state? The final chapter draws together the questions raised in each section and considers the implications of changes, and the relevance of particular social welfare and fiscal policies to contemporary family patterns.

Section 1:
The Family and the Home
Melanie Henwood

Changing patterns of employment of men and women, of domestic and caring responsibilities, and of the distribution of power within the family (if they are taking place) are likely to reflect broader change at the macro level of gender roles. Is the 'war between the sexes' still as pervasive as ever, or is there a move towards a 'truce' and a greater equality as some would argue.[1] Moreover, if there *is* now greater equality — or symmetry — to what factors might this be attributed? On a superficial level, at least, it is axiomatic that times change, but is such change more apparent than real?

In many ways it is a false distinction to consider household tasks separately from those concerned with child care. However, given its growing importance, the whole issue of caring for dependents (be these young children or disabled/elderly relatives) is fully discussed in Section Two. Similarly, the interaction of paid and unpaid work is crucial,[2] and the domestic division of labour needs to be considered in the context of market participation by women. (See Section Three.) We begin, however, with a consideration of responsibilities for housework.

As Ann Oakley pointed out in *The Sociology of Housework* in 1974[3], in domestic matters, "the general consensus of opinion is that husbands now participate much more than they used to". In contrast to this consensus, Oakley found "only a minority of husbands give the kind of help that assertions of equality in modern marriage imply". In particular, the home and children remained the women's primary responsibility.

Is there evidence of significant change in more recent years, and the emergence of more egalitarian or symmetrical relationships?

Sociological interest in the roles of men and women within marriage developed during the 1960s and 1970s. These earlier works (notably Young and Willmott's *'The*

Symmetrical Family'; and Fletcher's *The Family and Marriage*) emphasised the greater equality of the modern marriage. Elizabeth Bott's study of *Family and Social Network* (1957) devised the distinction between 'joint' and 'segregated' marriage roles.[4] Bott identified 'complementary', 'independent' and 'joint' modes in which all couples organised their activities — with variations in the relative amounts of each. Such work has since been criticised for methodological bias. In particular it was assumed that there would be a basic division of labour; jointness only assessed variations from this baseline.

The choice of domestic tasks included in any index of jointness is also highly significant. Most studies have concentrated on such areas as weekly shopping, washing up, putting children to bed and taking them out. As Oakley observes:

"These are highly selective questions, leaving out, as they do, cleaning, daily shopping, washing, ironing, cooking and the routine care of children (. . .). A number of studies (. . .) make it clear that of all domestic tasks, putting children to bed, taking children out, washing up and doing the main shopping are the ones most likely to be engaged in by men (. . .) a high level of male participation here is more acceptable than it is in other areas."

The domestic division of Labour: Theory and practice

Table 1: Domestic tasks and women's employment

		Full time working women %	Part time working women %
Household shopping:	Mainly man	4	4
	Mainly woman	52	64
	Shared equally	43	32
Preparation of evening meal:	Mainly man	11	4
	Mainly woman	61	79
	Shared equally	26	15
Household cleaning:	Mainly man	6	1
	Mainly woman	61	83
	Shared equally	33	15
Washing and ironing:	Mainly man	4	—
	Mainly woman	81	95
	Shared equally	14	5
Repairs of household equipment:	Mainly man	83	74
	Mainly woman	5	13
	Shared equally	12	11

Source: R. Jowell & S. Witherspoon (eds) *British Social Attitudes*. Gower. 1985. P.57.

As Table 1 indicates recent evidence shows that the employment status of wives affects the extent to which they perform domestic tasks traditionally associated with women at home. Working women are less likely than non-working to carry the entire responsibility for housework. However, as noted in the 1985 British Social Attitudes Survey (BSAS):

"Not that women working full time outside the home had an egalitarian division of domestic work: they were merely somewhat less unequal. And women with part time jobs outside the home had a particularly unequal division of labour, partly reflecting the fact that many women who worked part time also had young children." [6]

Martin and Roberts[7] have used the concept of a 'houseworker' to denote major domestic responsibility. This, they suggest, is anyone in the household responsible for at least half the domestic tasks. Some 99% of married women in their survey were thus defined ("so it was very rare for the husband to assume more than half the share of the domestic responsibilities").

"However only 46% of non-married women were houseworkers. Those women who were not houseworkers were generally living with their parents and were predominantly young single women. Among the non-married women only 25% of the single women were houseworkers compared with 93% of the widowed, divorced and separated. Altogether 88% of all women were houseworkers." [8]

Almost three quarters (73%) of wives in the Women and Employment survey[9] reported that they did all or most of the housework. Housework was more likely to be shared to some extent where wives were working full or part time:

"Nevertheless, even among women working full time 13% said that they did all the housework and 41% that they did most of it. So 54% of women working full time were combining paid work with the major share of housework at home." [10]

Very similar results then to those obtained in the British Social Attitudes Survey. As Airey has observed, "whether or not the contemporary British family is symmetrical in other respects, it is far from symmetrical in the allocation of household tasks."[11] The empirical evidence is that women are still largely responsible for day to day domestic and household chores, while men only play a greater role in the more traditionally 'masculine' area of household repairs. The 1985 BSAS found in 83% of all households the man was mainly responsible for repairing household equipment, with only 8% of couples sharing the task equally. Working women were more likely to share this chore, but even then it was relatively rare (12% of full time working women and 11% part time working women said they shared it equally).

How much equality *should* there be?

If — as it would seem — there is little equality in the kitchen, is this a major discontent among couples? Martin and Roberts point out that there are some difficulties in attempting to elicit satisfaction ratings within a structured interview ("people usually tend to give responses indicating that they are satisfied with their current situation"). Nonetheless, they report that wives were generally satisfied with the amount of work their husbands did (although 20% thought their husbands should do more). Similarly, most of the husbands thought that they did about the right amount (although 3% felt that they did too much and 20% that they did not do enough). The 1985 British Social Attitudes Survey found both men and women favoured a more equal division of labour than existed, although "the answers from both sexes were still far from egalitarian".

"Ideals were clearly tempered by current experience, as married men and women were less egalitarian (even prescriptively) than either the formerly married or the never married." [12]

Research by Brannen and Moss examined two parent households in which the women had returned to full time employment within 9 months of the birth of their first child, and where "husbands and wives were almost equal in terms of their employment attachment — jobs, hours and earnings". They still found a very unequal balance in domestic responsibilities. In the face of this, however, the women expressed "little overt dissatisfaction". Many of the women viewed their work as secondary to their husband's and were ambivalent about their own return to work:

"In such circumstances, women's criticisms of their partner's level of involvement and support were restrained, either because the women basically accepted that they should assume primary responsibility for child care and housework; or because feeling critical of their partner's contribution to child care and housework triggered or exacerbated personal doubts and guilt, which in turn muted, qualified or repressed altogether this criticism of others." [13]

The study found many examples of women who expressed a commitment to sharing domestic work equally. This principle was clearly breached in practice, and yet, as the authors observe, "they professed themselves to be relatively satisfied overall with their marriages and with husbands' support".

Equality and Marriage

The Social Attitudes Survey found married women

working full time had more egalitarian attitudes than either other married women or never married women. As the authors remark, those women who faced the greatest burden of household and employment responsibilities seemed the most dissatisfied with a traditional domestic division of labour.

Signs that attitudes and practices are changing might be sought among younger adults. Certainly the Social Attitudes Survey found those aged 18-24 "much more egalitarian than the general population". However, the determining variable was not so much youth per se, as marital status: The young unmarried — especially unmarried women — were considerably more egalitarian in their attitudes towards household tasks than were young married couples in their performance of them. It is the high proportion of unmarried individuals in this cohort (18-24) which lends its egalitarian character: "the pattern of answers from the married 18-24 year olds is not dissimilar to that of the general population."[14]

Table 2: Attitudes and practices in domestic equality among 18-24 year olds

		Preparation of evening meal	Household cleaning	Household shopping	Washing and ironing
Total married: task *is* shared equally	%	17	24	44	10
Married 18-24 task *is* shared equally	%	21	24	56	22
Total unmarried 18-24: task *should be* shared equally	%	51	60	68	31
Unmarried women 18-24: task *should be* shared equally	%	60	61	79	40

Source: R. Jowell & C. Airey (eds) *British Social Attitudes:* the 1984 report. Gower, 1984. P.135

Overall the picture is decidedly inegalitarian, and Airey remarks that it "is also probably similar to the pattern that would have been produced if we had asked the same questions in Britain at any time during the past thirty years or so".[15] This much is speculation — and certainly so in the absence of earlier comparative data. Nevertheless, the British findings were very similar to those of American data which *did* examine change between 1955 and 1971:

"Despite a substantial increase in women's employment in that period, household cleaning, washing dishes and shopping were still seen substantially as the wife's tasks. Indeed the 1971 data showed shopping to be even more exclusively a wife's task than it had been in 1955, while household repairs remained substantially the husband's job." [16]

Are we as equal as we think we are or claim to be?

Any self-reporting survey which is dependent on individuals' perceptions is subject to some bias. The Social Attitudes survey noted "subtle but consistent differences" between male and female respondents in their reports on the sharing of household tasks, such that men viewed the extent of their participation as greater than did their partners. Similarly, the Harris survey[17] found the majority of both husbands and wives thought that the husband had less involvement with a number of household chores than did 'the average man'.

Where does this leave the concept of the symmetrical family? Young and Willmott concede:

"Power has not been distributed equally in more than a few families. Division of labour is still the rule, with the husband doing the 'man's' work and the wife taking prime responsibility for the housekeeping and the children. (. . .) this applies to the majority of families . . ." [18]

Nonetheless, they maintain the 'direction of change' *is* towards a more blurred differentiation, with less rigid role segregation:

"These various historical processes are still working their way through the social structure which means that, in many if not all respects, they have had a fuller effect on the families of richer than poorer people, and of younger rather than older. With poorer and with older people the vestiges of stage 2 are still very much apparent (. . .) In stage 2 families there was segregation of roles in many

more ways than those to do with money. If husbands did any 'work' at all at home the tasks that they, and their wives, thought proper to them were those to which male strength and male manual skill lent themselves." [19]

They go on to suggest that although in the past "it was not a man's place to do women's work any more than the other way around. All that has now changed. Wives are working outside the home in what is much less of a man's world than it used to be." It is undoubtedly true that more women today work outside the home (see Section Three). But to infer that this alone signals massive change is misleading. As the research evidence indicates, most women combine paid work with the major share of housework. While it is true that men — on average — probably take a more active role in the home than in the past, this is typically a helping role rather than an egalitarian allocation of domestic responsibility.

Table 3: Occupational class and husband's help in the home

Reported help to wife at least once a week	Professional and managerial	Clerical	Skilled	Semi-skilled and unskilled	All
None	14%	13%	14%	24%	15%
Washing up only	16%	7%	13%	12%	13%
Other tasks (cleaning, cooking, child care etc.), with or without washing up	70%	80%	73%	64%	72%
Total %	100%	100%	100%	100%	100%
Number	171	70	236	107	585

Source: M. Young & P. Willmott: *The Symmetrical Family* (1973). Routledge & Kegal Paul, Table 8, P.95

It is also true, as Table 3 indicates, that the degree of cooperation varies by occupational class. Young and Willmott found that while husbands in the top (managerial and professional) group helped rather less with cleaning, considering all forms of help (washing up, cleaning, cooking, childcare etc) they helped out rather more than semi-skilled and unskilled workers. The principle of 'stratified diffusion' is invoked by Young and Willmott to explain this pattern: liberalisation of attitudes is argued to begin with the middle classes and gradually 'trickle downwards'.

If a trend towards greater equality in the home may be identified, it is equally true that most couples are still a long way off true egalitarianism or symmetry.

Young and Willmott had forecast that symmetry would be a continuing development:

"By the next century — with the pioneers of 1970 already at the front of the column — society will have moved from (a) one demanding job for the wife (i.e. in the home) and one for the husband (i.e. in paid work) through (b) two demanding jobs for the wife and one for the husband, to (c) two demanding jobs for the wife and two for the husband. The symmetry will be complete. Instead of two jobs there will be four." [20]

Admittedly we have not yet entered the 21st century, and further change may occur. However, the basis for the assumption of change (i.e. that men were "evidently back in the home") has itself been criticised. Ann Oakley's treatise on the sociology of housework argued that methodological bias over-stated the extent of male domesticity found by Young and Willmott. Moreover, their measure was only the extent to which men 'helped': the area of responsibility was still seen principally as the women's. Oakley suggests:

"In only a small number of marriages is the husband notably domesticated, and even where this happens, a fundamental separation remains: home and children are the women's primary responsibility. Doubt is cast on the view that marriage is an egalitarian relationship." [21]

Towards Greater Equality?

This section has examined the roles of men and women at home. What has emerged is a picture of home and hearth which is still very much a female domain. Where married women are in paid employment, there is more likely to be *some* sharing of domestic responsibilities by their husbands, but for most this is a long way from a truly egalitarian division.

Marriage itself appears to dilute liberal attitudes, and young married couples are very much less egalitarian in practice than are their single counterparts, in principle.

Research into newly weds reveals that even in the very early days of a marriage a pattern tends to emerge of husbands as primary breadwinners and their wives as secondary earners with major responsibility for domestic chores.[22] Such couples typically justify this arrangement by reference to *anticipation of parenthood*. As Brannen and Moss observe, "such findings are not inconsistent with those of other studies which have found that the onset of parenthood is marked by a clear division of domestic labour."[23]

Methodological difficulties impede accurate analysis over time. We have remarked on the problems associated with the task based empirical models, and moreover, without careful multi-variate analysis, findings will tend to be rather general. It is probable that there *is* a greater equality and more cooperation in the home today than previously, but the shift would seem to be one of degree rather than a fundamental change or widespread role reversal. Moreover, a greater equality of status and a greater sharing of other aspects of life (such as mutual interests and leisure activities within the modern 'companionate marriage') *need* not indicate domestic equality.

Oakley's conclusions in 1974 on marriage and the division of labour seem equally accurate observations on the most recent empirical data:

"Psychological intimacy between husband and wife, an intermingling of their social worlds, and a more equitable distribution of power in marriage are undoubtedly areas in which marriage in general has changed. But the importance of women's enduring role as housewives and as the main rearers of children continues." [24]

The same is true if we consider the extent to which women are sharing the traditional 'male' preserves within the home. Moreover, notwithstanding developments in dual earner households, it is largely true that most men still have the major responsibility of being the family breadwinner. These themes are further explored in Section Three.

Section 2: Family Care

Melanie Henwood

Child Care

Many studies of the domestic division of labour include child care alongside domestic tasks such as washing up or cooking. We treat it separately in order to consider the question of care more generally. Increasingly the caring role is not only concerned with the day to day tending of small children, rather it is associated with a life cycle of caring responsibilities. That is, caring for children, for elderly relatives, and finally for aged spouses.[1]

For feminists — and their critics — motherhood has been a central bugbear. Much of the analysis of the maternal role is equally applicable to this wider caring role. In its most simple form the feminist critique has challenged the 'biology as destiny' perspective, and the view which ascribes caring traits as distinguishing femininity:

"(. . .) the fact that the qualities demanded of caregivers — a sensitivity to the needs of others, an ability to wait, watch and adapt as these needs change — are the qualities displayed by women in Western society." [2]

Similarly, it has been pointed out:

"At least since the nineteenth century, motherhood has been glorified as women's chief vocation and central definition. The tie between mother and child has been exalted, and traits of nurturance, selflessness, and altruism have been defined as the essence of the maternal, and hence, of the womanly." [3]

The separation of reproduction and nurturing has been seen by some as the key to women's emancipation. Since the late 1960s and early 1970s initial questions about mothering have been raised, with the role being seen more broadly as 'parenting'.

Just as developments with contraceptives have signalled the possible separation of sexual relations and reproduction, similarly, the advent of safe feeding formulas no longer means the mother is necessarily tied to the care of her infant. While small children *do* need care, some would argue there is no physical reason why mothers or indeed women should provide it. Recent and well publicised developments in surrogacy and test tube babies may have also challenged many assumptions such as the irreplaceable nature of the biological mother-child bond.

Much feminist argument has emphasised the issue of choice in motherhood — both in whether or not to have children as much as in questions about child care. While the earliest analyses perhaps stressed the oppression of motherhood, later work however also emphasised the potential richness and rewards of mothering.

What, if anything, has been the impact of such thinking? Has the feminist emphasis on the personal experience as political made any difference to the everyday life of most families, and the way in which care especially is organised? Is there evidence that the caregivers of today have freely chosen their role and that nurturing is being shared much more equally with men?

Mothers and Fathers: Changing Roles?

If 'new men' are developing, so it might be expected are 'new fathers':

"(. . .) the man who is there at the birth, who 'bonds' with his baby, bathes it, changes nappies, is not afraid to express his tenderness or push a buggy. He may even swop roles with his wife and let her get back to work." [4]

Moreover some of these are discovering fatherhood late in life.

"(. . .) the man who leaves his first wife and teenage children (having been nowhere near the birth and never changed a nappy), then marries a much younger woman and goes enthusiastically into the birth-bath-and-potty routine. Many a balding figure now haunts Mothercare in his lunch-hour to the secret fury, no doubt of his ex-wife." [5]

The stereotype is easily drawn and recognised, but it is unclear how accurate it really is, or how widespread the phenomenon of 'the good father' so described, as opposed to the traditional model which defines 'father' almost exclusively in terms of main breadwinner and provider.

Are fathers today generally more likely to be equal partners in the care of their children, or is it still more usual for mothers to do most of the work, although with role reversals affecting an increasing minority? A recent book which reflected critically on the 'new father' observed that "Despite the wave of optimism driving contemporary accounts, the evidence for the existence of such a man is much less convincing."[6]

In discussing the domestic division of labour we have already noted that the British Social Attitudes Survey found households with young children displaying inegalitarian patterns ". . . with wives more likely to do most of the tasks, although men in such households were also slightly more likely than average to do some traditionally 'non-male' tasks like household shopping and the evening dishes."[7]

As noted in the previous section, some time-use studies in Britain have examined the division of domestic work within the home (such as work conducted by Young and Willmott). As Piachaud has pointed out, however, these have been very limited and have not provided any detailed information on child care. Piachaud recently attempted to redress this balance with a study examining the basic tasks of caring for children aged under 5.[8] These basic tasks (listed below) did not include time spent on 'educational and entertaining activities', nor on 'supervisory or on-call activities'. Concentration was on 'basic, largely inescapable tasks'. The time which might be allocated to the other types of activity omitted, Piachaud suggests, would be very much harder to quantify and he comments:

"But it must be acknowledged that the dividing line between these and the basic tasks is arbitrary and tasks that are crucial to mental development are in no way less important than the more physical set of basic tasks considered here." [9]

Looking after children is — in common with other domestic labour — physically onerous and tiring. The basic tasks entailed in this care were identified as:

- getting children up and dressed;
- toileting and changing nappies;

- taking children to childminder, nursery or school and collecting again;
- extra time for shopping;
- extra time for meals;
- washing and bathing;
- putting to bed;
- extra time for washing and ironing;
- clearing up and cleaning after children.

A sample of 55 respondents was selected on the basis of a door to door survey in a number of locations which identified households with at least one child under five years. In 89% of cases the household comprised (apart from children) the mother and her husband (or male partner). In 5.5% the mother was alone with the children, and in a further 5.5% another adult was present in addition to the mother and father. On the basis of these and other socio-economic characteristics it was felt that while the sample was not drawn from a random selection of a predetermined sampling frame, there was "no reason to believe it suffers from any serious bias".

Fifty hours a week

The total time spent in the specified child care tasks by mother, husband and other persons was established, as well as the distribution between different household members.

Overall,

"The most time-consuming task was, by a wide margin, feeding — including preparation of food, feeding or supervision of meals and washing up; this required an average of nearly two hours each day. Each of the other eight tasks took on average between half an hour and three quarters of an hour each day. In total, the nine tasks took on average 243 minutes, or just over seven hours per day." [10]

Not surprisingly more time was spent on basic care when there was a child aged under 2 (494 minutes on average compared with an average 376 minutes when the youngest child was aged 2 to 4).

"(. . .) it must be recognised that this is an awful lot of work. Most of the basic child care tasks are physically exhausting, repetitive and frequently boring and dirty.

Even when the mother had no other job the basic tasks occupied more hours than most men work in their jobs, and most of the mothers lacked any time free from child care responsibilities." [11]

Mothers and Fathers

Comparing time spent by different family members,

"By far the greater part of the time spent on child care tasks was spent by the mother — overall, 89% of the total time."

Even in households where the father was present, the mothers still provided 87% of basic care. Moreover, the fathers' share in total time did not differ significantly with the age of the youngest child.

The fathers' extent of involvement in care of their young children was based on the *mothers'* assessments, rather than from interviews with the men. However, other studies have shown a wide agreement between wives' and husbands' assessments of such situations. Moreover, as Piachaud remarks,

"Even a wide margin of under-estimation of fathers' time use would not alter the overwhelming inequality between mothers and fathers in time spent on basic child care tasks." [12]

The Women and Employment Survey (WES) also considered child care and reported women more likely to view child care as shared equally with their husbands than was the case with housework. 50% of wives felt their husbands took an equal share in child care, but only 26% thought they shared the housework equally. As with housework, however, women who were working (especially full time) were more likely than non-working women to see child care as shared.

The assessments made by some of the non-working women at home with young children, however, seemed to discount the time they spent caring for children while their husbands were out at work; their view of husbands sharing child care equally was based on the times when the husband was around the home. Husbands in the survey seemed to take account of this: disparities in the answers of husbands and non-working wives indicated

23

Table 4: Husbands' and Wives' views of child care

Views about share of child care	Wife's work status								Married women with children under 16	
	Working full time		Working part time		All working		Not working			
	Wife's view	Husband's view	Wife's view	Husband's view	Wife's view	Husband's view	Wife's view	Husband's view	Wife's view	Husband's view
	%	%	%	%	%	%	%	%	%	%
Wife does it all	5	2	8	5	7	4	11	6	9	5
Wife does most of it	24	24	36	44	32	39	48	64	40	51
Shared half and half	67	72	55	51	59	57	41	30	50	44
Husband does most of it	4	2	1	–	2	0	0	0	1	0
Husband does it all	0	–	–	–	0	–	–	–	0	–
	100	100	100	100	100	100	100	100	100	100
Base	370	63	867	158	1,237	221	1,119	191	2,366	414

Source: J. Martin & C. Roberts: *Women and Employment* HMSO 1984, Table 8.9

husbands' views that they did less in the way of child care than their wives credited them with. 41% of non-working wives thought their husbands shared half the work of child care. Only 30% of the husbands agreed with this, while some 64% thought their wife did most of such work.

The Survey also found mothers and fathers typically involved in different aspects of care.

"Wives were more likely to be involved in the routine basic care such as feeding, dressing, washing and so on, while husbands spent time playing with the children or taking them out." [13]

The finding that fathers' involvement in child care tends to be concentrated around the more enjoyable and less demanding aspects such as play and outings is consistent with earlier work by Oakley.[14] The 'good father' was viewed not as one who shared the physical labour of care, but as one who would "take the children off the mother's hands occasionally at weekends, to be generally interested in their well-being and to take over in times of crisis".[15] He plays with the children, but takes little routine responsibility.

Between both husbands and wives in the WES there was a high level of agreement that the husband's child care involvement was "about right". Overall this was true of 85% wives and 79% husbands, and of slightly higher proportions where the wife was working. Non-working wives are more likely to have very young children and might therefore feel in need of more help from their husbands. Martin and Roberts comment that the general satisfaction on the part of wives probably also reflects an expectation that their husband's contribution to child care will be limited.

Universal Press Syndicate © 1986 GB Trudeau

Mr Average?

The Harris 'Britons Observed' survey asked husbands and wives whether they/their husband did more of a range of household chores than 'the average man does'. On this basis, Mr Average would score 50% every time: women's views of their husband's participation in looking after children registered 19% while husbands' own views scored 16%. Why this figure should be so much below 'the average' may be due to two factors:

"a) because wives and husbands have an inflated view of the average and compare their own households unfavourably; and/or b) because the concept of the average is very vague, and what people are really saying is that they have low expectations in their own household of what the husband should do . . ." [16]

Without time series data it is difficult to know how — if at all — this pattern has altered. While mothers *do* still take the major responsibility for the care of young children, there is a 'sense' of fathers having more involvement than previously. There has been no study of paternal involvement over many years, and comparisons over brief time spans are contradictory. As Lewis and O'Brien suggest:

"It seems most likely that change in fathering roles has been restricted to particular areas of family life." [17]

For example there is evidence of greater involvement of fathers at the time of birth "but little difference in the performance of chores like nappy changing or bathing the baby". Another difficulty in assessing real change is the tendency to assume that historically fathers were more remote. Lewis and O'Brien suggest that "in each generation some authors feel that men are breaking new ground", and they quote Dybwad who comments:

"(. . .) while some authors see today's father as less active and further removed from the family, others quite to the contrary observe that he has found his way back to the family and shares actively and creatively many activities with wife and children. Apparently it depends on the author's vantage point whether and in what areas he discerns progress." [18]

Overall, however, the empirical evidence indicates that it

is mothers who remain most involved in the day to day care of their children.

Universal Press Syndicate © 1986 GB Trudeau

Child care and Employment

While the presence of young children in a family has no effect on fathers' economic activity rates, it is the single most important factor influencing whether or not women work, or whether they do so full or part time. (See Section Three.)

The time costs of child care typically result in foregone earnings for the caring parent. A number of factors interact to increase the likelihood that it will be mothers' rather than fathers' employment which is interrupted and earnings lost.

Piachaud argues that differences between men and women in training, experience and job interruptions "can be understood only in terms of the sexual division of parenting".

"(. . .) it is mothers who bear the brunt of basic child care tasks. This in turn leads to the self-perpetuation of sex inequalities. Since women commonly interrupt employment to look after children, they are given less training and acquire less experience than men, which results in their lower pay. If a family is then faced with the issue of whether the mother or father should reduce their paid work, it may make financial sense for the mother with a lower hourly pay, to stay at home — and this then reinforces the vicious circle of sex inequalities still further." [19]

Whatever egalitarian principles a couple may start out

with, it is likely therefore that they are often forced to bow to more pragmatic considerations.

As later sections show, husbands — whether parents or not — are more likely than wives to work long hours. These hours may also be irregular and for many involve time away from home. There are clear strains between family and working life, as a 1983 report from the Equal Opportunities Commission observed:

"As a man's identity has traditionally been based on his work outside the home, any efforts to assume more of a family role can result in increased tensions in the work situation. Time demanded by the family often conflicts directly with work commitments. Ironically it is at the period in the life cycle when fathers of young children desire to become more involved with their family, that work is likely to make excessive demands on their time." [20]

Lewis and O'Brien suggest that "in most societies material provision is the embodiment of male parenting". The 'job description' of the father's role within the home is arguably less clear than for the mother, and under such circumstances the 'fatherhood mandate' is one which is concentrated *outside of the home*.

"The fatherhood mandate, which encourages a consolidation and development of men's position in the public sphere of work, seems to bring more gains than losses. Absence from the home allows some freedom from domesticity, especially the dreary and repetitive aspects of housework and children. The energy devoted to a work role at one and the same time enhances the self professionally and financially while also providing the family with social status and financial support." [21]

Other research has also found fathers reporting high levels of work-home conflict. Typically these were middle class fathers subscribing to principles of shared family responsibilities while being heaviy involved in their work and relatively remote from domestic life.[22] Further analysis of the nature of the conflict experienced by such fathers suggests most would like to spend more time in the *company* of their small children, rather than have greater responsibility for child care or domestic work.[23]

A Vicious Circle

The worlds of employment and the home then form a complex and pervasive dialectic: women are usually principal carers because the loss of their employment is less significant than that of the male breadwinner; women remain lower paid and in poorer jobs because employers and prospective employers expect that women will leave to have children and will be unreliable as workers when young children are at home. As Piachaud concludes:

"There seems little doubt that sex equality of pay and equal opportunities in the labour market are unattainable given the asymmetrical family and the existing inequalities of child care and parenting." [24]

Martin and Roberts have similarly remarked that the differential position of men and women in the labour market is partly due to "their differing balance of home and paid work". The WES found husbands more likely to do more housework (as we have already noted) and child care when their wives also worked. Nonetheless, women remained responsible for the lion's share of such work. The tensions between work and domestic responsibilities are typically resolved by women through the adoption of part time work, although interestingly the part time option is far less common in other European countries than in Britain.

The 'cost' of having a child therefore represents very much more than the purely financial expenses incurred (considerable though these may be).[25] Opportunity costs (that is earnings and prospects foregone) need also to be considered. Piachaud argues that the time costs of young children and their consequences (particularly associated earnings losses) "have important implications for both the public provision of child care and for the level and structure of child benefits." [26]

Caring for other dependants

As we noted earlier, caring responsibilities are not confined solely to the care of young children, rather a *cycle of caring* is an increasing pattern. Recent years have seen a growing interest in 'informal carers', that is persons who care on a daily basis (sometimes around the clock) for a dependent individual (typically but not necessarily a relative) who would not be able to manage without that care.

Many of the questions relating to the provision of such care are similar to those concerning child care.

The demography of demand for care

In addition to normal caring demands made by young children are those arising from special needs such as: children with disabilities, adults with disabilities or chronic or serious illnesses, and frail elderly persons. The demography of such needs has been delineated most fully in relation to elderly people.[27] The ageing of the population is striking. Since the turn of the century advances in medical science, nutrition, public health, standards of housing and work conditions, have all contributed to reducing overall mortality and increasing the numbers and proportions of those living well into retirement.

It is the *ageing of the elderly population itself* which is now especially significant. To give just one example, while in 1901 a mere 57,000 people in Britain were aged 85 or over, by the time of the 1981 Census this had reached 552,000. By the turn of the next century these numbers will roughly double again to pass the million mark.[28]

Community Care Policy

Alongside such trends have been policy developments which — influenced in part by the rising costs of residential care — have sought to maintain such individuals in their own homes, 'in the community' for as long as possible. As the 1981 White Paper 'Growing Older' stated:

"Whatever level of public expenditure proves practicable, and however it is distributed, the primary sources of support and care for elderly people are informal and voluntary. These spring from the personal ties of kinship, friendship and neighbourhood. They are irreplaceable. It is the role of public authorities to sustain and, where necessary, develop — but never to displace — such support and care. Care in the community must increasingly mean care by the community."[29]

We have noted elsewhere that the implicit assumptions behind this statement indicate a belief in the primary responsibilities of the family in general, and of women as carers in particular.[30]

The majority of elderly people are fit and healthy and able to lead independent lives. Audrey Hunt's 1976 survey on the elderly at home found 0.3% elderly people permanently bedfast, and 4.2% housebound.[31] The 1985 report by the Audit Commission on managing social services for the elderly suggested around 18 per 1,000 elderly people comprised a small but significant proportion with very severe physical incapacities.[32] The minority of very frail elderly people represents the extreme end of a continuum of needs for assistance with daily life. Given the numerical increase in the elderly population this minority in greatest need is a growing one. The application of Hunt's findings to the current elderly population indicates 1,100,000 *severely* disabled elderly people — an increase of more than 100,000 since 1976. A further 2 million are moderately disabled.

The incidence of disability and handicap in the community is not, of course, restricted to the population aged over 65. Up to date information on disability and incapacity is not available, but a forthcoming OPCS Survey on disablement will provide further data. Townsend's national representative sample survey[33] in the late 1960s suggested 12% of the population have "a marked or specific disablement condition" and indicated at least 1.9 million people appreciably, severely or very severely incapacitated at the time of the survey (1968-69). This estimate did not include children under ten years old and data on the numbers of disabled children needing special care are less available. In a recent review of research evidence[34] Parker concluded that the numbers of children with severe impairment were between 89,000 and 126,000 (6.2 per 1,000 population). Moreover,

"all indications are that the population of children with severe disabilities has increased as more have survived infancy...." [35]

The future is uncertain. On the one hand, improved ante natal care and screening may reduce the numbers of handicapped live births,

"(...) on the other hand, improvements in medical

technology which save the lives of low birth-weight babies may contribute to an increase in the number of surviving, disabled, babies." [36]

Considering both the elderly and non-elderly populations together then it is very difficult, as Parker has remarked, to estimate with any certainty the numbers in the community requiring special care — or to be sure of the likely changes in this population. On the basis of the data which does exist the Equal Opportunities Commission has suggested that the total number of handicapped people who are at present living at home and needing care exceeds 1.5 million.[37]

Who Cares?

The research evidence indicates that women are most often the *principal* carers of such persons, and indeed are often sole carers receiving little or no support from other relatives, friends and neighbours, or organised services.[38]

Hunt's study of women's employment in the mid-1960s found 5% women aged 16-64 responsible to a greater or lesser extent for at least one elderly or infirm person *within* the household and 6% for one *outside* of the household.[39] In a subsequent survey of the Home Help service Hunt suggested that between the ages of 35-64 roughly one half of all housewives could expect to provide some help to elderly or infirm persons.[40]

Further evidence has been provided by more recent research. The Women and Employment data indicated 13% of all women had caring responsibilities for sick or elderly dependents, and this was true of more than one in five women aged over 40. Some 24% of these carers lived with the person for whom they were caring; a further 24% saw the person every day. Only 6% saw the dependent person less than once a week. The demands made by such responsibilities were equally evident in the hours spent caring:

- 26% reported constant attention
- 13% at least 15 hours a week
- 21% less than 5 hours a week.

As Martin and Roberts remark, "for some the amount of care they undertook was quite considerable and for a sizeable minority affected whether they could undertake paid work at all or the kind of work they could do."[41]

Carers are *predominantly* women

Research by the Equal Opportunities Commission found 75% carers of elderly or handicapped persons were women.[42] Other research has found the figure to be as high as 85%. Research also suggests that the caring experience is qualitatively different for men and women (with men likely to receive more support and at an earlier stage).

Reviewing the research Parker has concluded:

"The evidence then, is unequivocal. While the family, where it exists, still cares for its elderly members within the family, it is wives, daughters, daughters-in-law and other female relatives who shoulder the main burden of responsibility. Moreover, when the carer has taken on the burden she is likely to receive little practical support from other relatives." [43]

Unshared Care

The lack of shared care between men and women within families is particularly striking. A small scale study of family care of handicapped elderly persons[44] found husbands' attitudes to their wives' caring activities distant or neutral:

"They tended to live their own lives and not get involved in caring for the elderly relative: two went on separate holidays; most got immersed in their work, and in the evenings many went to a pub. Life for these families was highly segregated, with little if any sharing." [45]

Well over half the husbands played no direct role in care, and indeed for every minute that husbands who did take an active part spent on primary care activities, their wives expended nineteen.

"for the families in the sample, the idea of a symmetrical family with both partners sharing tasks and having more or less equal rights had little reality." [46]

As in the case of domestic responsibilities it is interesting to compare such practices with aspirations. The 1984 British Social Attitudes Survey obtained reactions to the statement that "children have an obligation to look after their parents when they are old". Overall, 39% of respondents agreed with this and 33% disagreed (with some 21% having no strong feelings one way or the other). However,

"the most consistent (and surprising) difference that emerges is between men and women — rather than between old and young — on children's obligations towards their parents. Men in all age groups are more likely than women in the same age groups to support the statement." [47]

The Harris 'Britons Observed' survey similarly asked whether elderly persons not in need of hospital care but unable to live totally independently should move in with younger household members. Men were more likely to support this proposal than women (25% and 15% respectively). A stated willingness to give up a job to look after an elderly parent rather than see them enter residential care was also surprising:

"we were staggered that 51% said they would, and frankly incredulous that 32% of men said so." [48]

The data certainly suggest such incredulity has some foundation.

A very similar profile is presented by the pattern of care for other groups (although there is less research data available on children and non-elderly adults with physical disabilities). As in most families with 'normal' children, the majority of care for a disabled or chronically sick child is provided by the mother. Where fathers *do* make a contribution it is often with the easier and more time limited aspects (again, as with healthy children).

'Community care' then is typically a by-word for 'family' care; family care — in turn — generally equals care by women.[49]

One reason why this clear sexual division should be of importance is the association between caring and poverty. Hilary Graham has suggested these, are indeed, two sides of the same coin: "Caring is what they do; poverty describes the economic circumstances in which they do it".[50] The fact that caring is often a full time and unpaid task places many women in a position of economic dependency:

"Unlike other family dependents — children, for example, or a frail parent or a disabled spouse — women are economically dependent not because they need care but because they give it (. . .). For children and for men, it seems, economic dependency is the cost of being cared for; for women, economic dependency is the cost of caring." [51]

For many women this dependency will be upon a partner's earnings, which will not necessarily provide any protection from poverty. Some aspects of intra household economic inequalities are further explored in Section Four.

Natural, right and best?

As with childcare and domestic work generally, the largely inegalitarian organisation of family care does not, however, emerge as a highly contentious issue in the research.

Nissel and Bonnerjea's study[52] of people caring for elderly dependents found in most cases that women's attitudes to caring responsibilities closely underlined traditional caring roles. As one respondent commented:

"Well, I don't expect my family to do my job, let's put it that way. If I'm unwell, then they will do it, they'll just do it spontaneously. But if I'm well, I wouldn't want them to be doing it because I'm quite happy doing it myself." [53]

The apparent satisfaction with these inegalitarian arrangements indicates, as Moss has commented, that the present organisation of care within the family owes not solely to economic expediency or other pragmatic considerations such as we have discussed, "but above all (to) the still widely held ideological view that this arrangement is natural, right and best."[54]

In the following section we examine paid work and the patterns which this takes for men and women. The rise of the dual worker household is particularly significant. Role reversal couples (in which the wife is employed and the husband economically inactive) are, however, very rare.

Elsewhere — for instance in Australia; the USA; Sweden, and Israel — such couples have been the subject of much more research and media interest than in Britain.

Some research shows fathers taking a major responsibility for child care, but Graeme Russell[55] has argued that this "does not necessarily lead to fathers assuming the overall responsibility for children in the way that traditional mothers do". Equally, men's unemployment does not necessarily change couples' views about traditional male household jobs or breadwinner responsibility. The circumstances which lead to a woman working while her husband is at home may be viewed by couples as a temporary aberration rather than a long term and fundamental change.

The reasons for changing roles which couples offer to researchers include family, financial, and employment conditions (for example, if the husband loses his job or the wife can earn more) as well as egalitarian beliefs about the roles of men and women. In Sweden where parents have the same leave options from employment clearly not *all* reverse roles, and it may be only "fathers who are highly motivated and who have confidence in their skills, who will respond to changes in policies."[56]

Some (in fact most) of the role reversal families have been found to revert sooner or later, to more traditional patterns, and for many this will again reflect changed employment and financial conditions which no longer make the arrangement attractive. It is likely that there are also considerable social pressures on couples to revert to traditional patterns.

Section 3: Paid Work

Lesley Rimmer

". . . I think it is important to emphasise the role of ideology in constraining the work practices and divisions of labour of women both inside and outside the household. If the divisions of labour are changing, it is no bad thing to recognise that such change has been the normal pattern of things for the last two hundred years. It is unlikely that change of the pattern of work between men and women will cease or that some utopian steady state situation will ever emerge. The complexity of the dialectic is too full of contradictions." [1]

The previous sections have considered the organisation of domestic and caring responsibilities, and in particular the division of these between men and women. This section now turns to focus on the division of paid employment and the experience of unemployment between men and women in families. As the previous sections have shown, the ability to participate in the paid labour market depends crucially on the demands of, and involvement in, non-paid domestic work, and the care of dependants. The differential demands of domestic work explain in large part the differentials in employment participation and in hours of paid work between men and women, and the patterns we describe cannot be understood without this in mind.

We analyse first the different patterns of paid employment in families of different types, and consider how these have changed over time. We then turn to unemployment and examine how far the unemployment of one partner affects that of the other, and indeed its broader impact upon the family. Finally we consider briefly men's and women's attitudes to one another's employment.

Male and Female Economic Activity

Although there has been a rapid increase in women's participation in paid work over the last two decades men are, overall, still much more likely than women to be in

Table 5: Women's economic activity by life cycle stage

Economic activity	Life cycle stage							
	Childless women aged:		Women with youngest child aged:			Women with all children aged 16 and over, aged:		All women except full time students
	Under 30	30 or over	0-4	5-10	11-15	Under 50	50 or over	
	%	%	%	%	%	%	%	%
Working full time	82	67	7	16	31	40	27	35
Working part time	3	12	20	48	45	37	32	28
Total working	**85**	**79**	**27**	**64**	**76**	**77**	**59**	**63**
'Unemployed'	11	6	4	4	5	5	5	6
Total economically active	**96**	**85**	**31**	**68**	**81**	**82**	**64**	**69**
Economically inactive	4	15	69	32	19	18	36	31
	100	**100**	**100**	**100**	**100**	**100**	**100**	**100**
Base	887	414	1,038	868	710	468	910	5,295

Source: J. Martin & C. Roberts: *Women and Employment*. DE/OPCS, HMSO 1984. Table 2.11

paid employment. In 1984 the economic activity rate for males aged 16-64 was 88% and 61% for married women aged 16-59. Married women have lower economic activity rates than non-married women (67% of whom were economically active in 1983), but this is primarily an effect of the presence of children and not marital status per se.[2]

Motherhood and Employment

Whereas in previous generations women tended to give up work on marriage, the first major interruption to most women's paid employment — if the current high levels of youth unemployment are set aside — now comes at the birth of the first child. As the previous section discussed, women's involvement in paid work is particularly low when they have a child aged under five in the household, and tends to increase with the age of the youngest child.

Table 5 shows that 96% of childless women under 30 (excluding full-time students) are economically active, compared to just 31% of women with a youngest child aged under five. The percentage economically active rises to 81% for women with a youngest child aged 11-15 and 82% for women under 50 whose youngest child is 16 or over. It then appears to decline again as women age, although part of this may be a cohort or generational effect (that is, it may not be a pattern among subsequent cohorts of women who pass their fiftieth birthday).

The Table also shows that the effect of children on a woman's participation is not simply whether or not she works, but in particular whether she works full or part time. Women with children are much more likely than their childless counterparts to work part-time and some 70% of mothers do so.[3]

The impact of children on fathers' participation is far less dramatic. Four out of ten of the male labour force have dependent children but this has virtually no impact on their participation rate. For example, the 1982 General Household Survey showed that the husband was working in 88% of those couples with dependent children. In fact, Moss has argued that men tend to work *longer* hours when they have young children, in contrast to women whose hours of paid work are reduced.[4] Indeed this is not so surprising. If a woman who has previously worked no longer does so when she has young children, the family will experience a fall in income at the very time when its needs and expenses are increasing, and the attraction of paid overtime for the husband will often be significant. The *number* of children does, however, seem to have some impact, with lower levels of economic activity for fathers with four or more children.[5]

The pattern of employment within couples then, differs with their age and by the presence or absence of children. In 1982 for example, in 80% of childless couples in which the wife was under 30 both partners were working, compared to just 59% where the wife was aged 30-59,[6] and 54% of all couples (with and without children). Only 47% of couples with dependent children had two earners in 1984, while both partners worked in 61% of all married couples of working age (ie with and without children).

Dual Earner Households

The rise in women's paid work has meant the rise of the dual earner household. The Women and Employment Survey (WES), for example, showed that in 1980 in 57% of couples, husbands and wives were both working. If partners who were unemployed were included, the proportion of couples where both were economically active rose to 62%. The second most common pattern — but far less common than policy makers often assume — was the one earner couple, where the husband worked and his wife was economically inactive; this accounted for 31% of couples. The proportion of couples with other combinations of employment status is very small. In the WES 2% of husbands and wives were both economically inactive, and most of these tended to be older couples. There was also a small proportion (2%) of role reversal couples where the wife worked and her husband was economically inactive. These also tended to be older couples.[7]

Similar evidence comes from the 1984 General Household Survey which found 57% of couples with both partners working; 33% where the husband worked and the wife did not; 4% where the wife was working, and the husband was unemployed or economically inactive, and 9% where neither husband nor wife were working.[8]

Men and Women's hours of work

It is clear then that husbands are more likely to undertake paid work than their wives. They are also much more likely to work longer hours. The overwhelming majority of husbands in the WES sample worked full time, whereas only 27% of wives were in full time employment and 33% worked part time. On average husbands worked 45.1 hours per week (including overtime), but even women who worked full time averaged only 37.4 hours per week. Indeed only 4% of wives worked longer hours than their husbands and 11% worked the same number of hours. Thus in 85% of cases husbands worked longer hours than their wives, reflecting both the higher incidence of part time working amongst wives and the shorter hours worked by full time working wives (and the lesser likelihood of their working overtime).[9]

It is not clear whether wives' and husbands' hours of work can be regarded as substitutable (that is, whether husbands work more if their wives are unable to). Certainly the WES found husbands of women working full time worked the shortest hours — 43.9 hours on average — compared to husbands of non-working wives or husbands whose wives worked part time, who worked 44.7 and 46.4 hours a week on average respectively. However, not all hours of work are flexible, and paid overtime is rarely available in non-manual jobs.[10]

The experience of family life will be affected not only by how much men and women — husbands and wives, mothers and fathers — engage in paid work, but the times of day at which they do so. How far do couples arrange their paid work to allow themselves time together, or with their children? In 1973 Young and Willmott suggested that the gain for family symmetry had been a loss for home-centredness (with both sexes spending more time out at work and less at home), and that the door between the worlds of home and life was "a revolving one, men coming in, women going out."[11] Is this the case?

Flexible Working Hours & Domestic Responsibility

While there is little direct evidence on the working behaviour of couples, some insights can be gained from the pattern of women's working hours. If we assume that a standard working day starts before 10am and finishes at 4pm or later, but before 6pm, then overall 74% of full time women workers work this pattern (see Appendix 1 for definitions). As is to be expected, far fewer part timers work this pattern — only some 12%, with a corresponding increase in morning working (29% work hours beginning before 10am and finishing before 2pm), short days and evening working.

Such patterns are clearly related to domestic responsibilities, and to the availability of child care. For example, whereas the WES found only 1% of childless women under 30 who worked full time worked nights, this was true of 10% of full time workers with a child under five. Similarly twice as many of the latter group worked late days (6%) as the former.

Where part timers are concerned the patterns are even more complex: 38% of part time working women with a pre-school aged child working evenings (indeed, 78% of part time evening workers are mothers of children under 16), and 6% working nights.

Child Care Arrangements

Who provides child care for women working various patterns of hours? In most groups of part time women workers, the WES found husbands were most likely to look after the children while the wife was working (followed by grandmothers and other family members). Husbands provided such care for 90% of those part timers working evening shifts, and for a surprisingly high 57% of those working mornings.[12] While such arrangements obviously facilitate both partners working, and perhaps also enable both to share in the care of young children, they do so at the expense of reducing the time couples spend together, and this would appear to be particularly the case for couples with pre-school aged children.

Changing Patterns of Work

How have working patterns changed over time? One of the most significant developments is in the length of the working life, for both men and women.

Early Retirement

For men, perhaps one of the most notable changes in recent years has been in the level of 'early retirement'. Even before unemployment began to increase rapidly there were signs of a significant decline in the economic activity of older people. For men, as Table 6 below demonstrates, economic activity for those aged 65 and over fell from 19% in 1973 to 15% in 1979, and to just 9% by 1983. For married women in the same age group it halved from 8% in 1973 to 4% in 1983.

The latter end of the working life has also seen some dramatic declines. For *non-married* women aged 55 to 59, for example the decline was from 69% to 53% over the period and for men in that age group from 94% to 85%. Interestingly *married* women in this age group have *increased* their economic activity rate from 48% to 52%, and women in the next age group, 60-64, have hardly reduced their economic activity at all, in comparison to other groups.

Table 6: Economic activity by age and sex

	1973	1975	1979	1980	1981	1982	1983
Persons aged 16 or over							
Men							
55-59	94	94	88	89	90	90	85
60-64	85	84	75	67	73	64	63
65 & over	19	16	15	12	11	10	9
Non-married women							
55-59	69	62	61	64	61	64	53
60-64	34	34	23	26	23	18	17
65 & over	6	6	5	4	4	5	4
Married women							
55-59	48	49	55	52	54	52	52
60-64	25	26	25	25	21	22	20
65 & over	8	6	6	6	5	5	4

Source: OPCS Monitor GHS 1984/1

Extended working lives

At another level, however, it can be seen that for women especially, the length of working life is increasing in younger cohorts. Since women's employment has risen overall in recent years, women currently in their 30s or

40s have worked for a greater proportion of the time available than women now in their 50s would have done at those ages. On the basis of this, and on the restrictive assumption that there is no further rise in women's employment, it is expected that women currently in their early 40s will have worked for 63% of their potential working life up to age 60 while women in their early 30s can be expected to have worked for 67% of their lives by that age. Women now in their late 50s, on the other hand have only worked some 59% of their lives.[13]

Returning to Work

Women are also returning to work earlier after childbirth. The median time of return to work after the latest birth has fallen from 7.7 years for women with a latest birth in 1950-54 to 3.4 years for women with a latest birth in 1975-79.[14] Or to put it another way, whereas only 13% of mothers having a first birth in 1950-54 had returned to work within one year, and 20% had done so within 2 years, the corresponding figures for 1970-74 were 22% and 30% respectively.[15] The Women and Employment survey largely attributed these changes over time to the increasing proportions of women returning initially to part time work.

In the future however the high levels of unemployment we are experiencing may cause this period to lengthen again to some extent. It could also affect the proportion of women's working lives in which they are actually working, particularly for young workers experiencing a protracted period of unemployment after leaving school.

Unemployment within Families

The rise in unemployment in recent years has already been mentioned. With more than three million people officially unemployed, the numbers are certainly significant. Moreover, unemployment is not something which affects only individuals. There is growing evidence that unemployment concentrates within families.

It might be expected that families in which the male household head is out of work would be *more* likely to have a wife working. However, unemployed married men are *less* likely to have available a wife's earnings as a safety net to their unemployment than those who are employed. The DHSS cohort study of men entering unemployment in 1978, for example, showed that in the week prior to the husband's registration about one third of the cohort wives were in employment compared to more than half of all wives.[16] This confirms earlier work on the 1971 census[17] and the later analysis of the Women and Employment Survey. This showed that 62% of the wives of working husbands worked, compared with just 33% of the wives of unemployed men, and 40% of the wives of economically inactive men.[18] In addition, also in line with other findings, the wives of unemployed men were more likely to be unemployed than the wives of either working or economically inactive men: 12% of such wives were unemployed compared with 4% for the other two groups.

While this comparison between the economic status of husbands and wives in employed and unemployed families is both important in terms of inequalities between families, and of interest in itself, we are more concerned here with the relationship between husband and wife. How far does the unemployment of one partner affect that of the other?

The DHSS cohort study did show some effect of a husband's unemployment on the employment status of his wife. While few wives moved out of employment in the first month of their husband's unemployment (2%) slightly more (3%) moved into employment.[19] Some wives changed the number of hours they worked, with more increasing than decreasing their hours. Four months later 7% of wives not previously in work had moved into work, and 5% had moved out.

There is thus no *strong* confirmation of a tendency for husbands and wives to move into and out of employment together, although the proportion of working wives declined in successive stages of the study where husbands were still unemployed.[20]

Analysis of the Family Finances and Family Resources Surveys did not produce a clear picture either. In families where the husband had been continuously unemployed in the twelve months between the surveys, more wives joined the labour force than left it. Interestingly, similar proportions of wives joined the labour force in families where the husband moved into work as in those where the husband became unemployed.[21]

On balance the research does suggest some "discouragement" of wives from working, when their husband becomes unemployed. The explanation of this situation, however, is complex. Joshi analysed the reasons which wives of unemployed men gave for themselves leaving employment. Only 17% said that their husband's employment position affected their own work behaviour, and one fifth of these had joined the labour force. Among those who left work the need to care for their husband, who in some cases would be in poor health, was an important one.[22]

Attitudes of Husbands and Wives to Employment

While it is increasingly common for both partners to work outside the home, this may sometimes be a source of contention. The traditional view that "a woman's place is in the home" is rarely heard quite so blatantly these days. Nevertheless, such attitudes survive in a diluted form at least in some quarters.

We have already seen that while women are generally spending a greater part of their lives in paid employment, they also still carry the major burden of domestic and caring responsibilities. It might be expected that both these women and their husbands will have particular attitudes towards women's employment. In addition, some impression of how such attitudes might be changing is available from earlier survey data.

In Hunt's 1965 survey of Women's Employment, for example, 14% of wives were said to be "working in the teeth of their husband's disapproval".[23] By 1979 Marsh's survey of attitudes towards shift work in inner city communities showed that only 2% of husbands actively discouraged their wives from working.[24] On the other hand only 10% of husbands encouraged their wives, while the vast majority — 67% — agreed that the choice was left to the wife's judgement.

In the Women and Employment survey a more detailed analysis was undertaken, which captured some of the complexity of the domestic decision making process and the interaction with more generally held beliefs. In general husbands held more traditional views about home and work than wives (although the husbands of working wives were less traditional in outlook).

Although only 25% of women agreed that "a woman's place is in the home", some 46% agreed that "a husband's job is to earn the money; a wife's job is to look after the home and family". As Martin and Roberts point out, this need not be incompatible with thinking that women should have paid work as well, indeed some 55% disagreed with the view that "women can't combine a career and children". Moreover, the idea that married women have a *right* to work "whatever their family situation" attracted considerable support, although as might be expected, working and non-working women, and women with and without children, had rather different attitudes.

"The overall picture conveyed by these results is that only a minority of women nowadays hold to the traditional view that 'a woman's place is in the home'; although most endorse the right and need of married women with families to work, work is considered by many women to be secondary to home and family and something to be accommodated to domestic demands." [25]

When it came to their own situation 14% of wives working full time felt that their husband would prefer them not to work, while 52% felt that he was pleased that they did so. On the other hand 40% of non working women felt their husband preferred them not to work, while 14% suspected he would be pleased if they did.

This apparent consensus for all but a minority was confirmed by an analysis of husbands' and wives' responses to the same statements. Over half the wives gave identical answers to their husbands while for only around 10% was there complete disagreement.[26] Overall the survey suggested that regardless of their family situation husbands were more likely to endorse their wife working if she was working, and to endorse her being at home if she was not working. But family circumstances were an important factor: husbands of wives with dependent children were generally less likely to be very supportive of their working wives, and more likely to endorse home oriented views than husbands of childless wives, or with children over 16.

We noted above that general attitudes to women working varied with their differing family responsibilities, and some idea of the changes can be gained from a comparison of the WES with Hunt's 1965 data. Certainly this indicated some change over time. In 1965 only 13%

of women felt that a childless married woman *ought* to work if able to do so; by 1980 some 33% shared this view. Similarly in 1965 there was little support for the idea that women with children should have a right to work if they wanted. Some 35% supported this where children were of school age, but only 5% where pre-school children were involved; by 1980 the proportions had risen to 50% and 15% respectively.

"Though marked, the changes are not revolutionary; 60% of women felt mothers of pre-school children should stay at home." [27]

The 1985 report of the British Social Attitudes Survey also considered attitudes to women's employment. Using the same statements as had the WES in 1980 this survey found notably less traditionalist attitudes among women. For example, in 1984 only 27% of women agreed that in times of high unemployment married women should stay at home, compared to 35% in the WES data. Similarly while in 1980 46% of women agreed that it was the husband's job to earn money and the wife's to care for the home and family, this view was subscribed to by only 32% in the later survey.[28]

That there *has* been some change in the views both of men and women is not surprising given the increase in women's economic activity over the period. We have seen that in general however work still takes second place to the demands of children and home. As Martin and Roberts remark, this shift in attitude matches the increase of married women's *part time* rather than full time employment over the same period.

In part these attitudes will reflect the family's financial situation, and the actual or potential contribution of the wife's earnings. The WES evidence underlined the financial importance of work to *most* women; 65% of both husbands and wives disagreed with the view that married women's earnings were pin money and that they didn't really *need* a job.[29] It is to such financial issues that we now turn.

Section 4:
Income and Resources
Lesley Rimmer

"As long ago as my own childhood I remember George Bernard Shaw writing to the press to ridicule this system, asserting that for his part he was quite unable to complete his income tax return as he had no idea of his wife's income, although to judge from her style of living it appeared to be considerable." [1]

The focus of this chapter is the allocation and control of major finances and resources inside the family. This is an area of emerging policy interest. Certainly it is one which arouses controversy. The eventual defeat of proposals to replace Family Income Supplement (usually paid to mothers) with Family Credit through the husband's pay packet, as part of the 1986 Social Security Bill, highlighted some of these issues. It is equally central to the question of transferable tax allowances for married couples, the subject of a Green Paper in 1986.

Until recently, however, it has been a relatively neglected area for researchers and policy makers alike, with questions of the financial arrangements after divorce (maintenance payments and the distribution of matrimonial property) having received more public attention than arrangements *within* marriage. Renewed emphasis on this issue is evident in the recent Law Commission Report on the Transfer of Money Between Spouses in relation to the Married Women's Property Act, 1964.[2]

Here we largely limit the range of issues discussed to the relative contribution of husbands and wives to family income; and to patterns of money management within marriage and other long term relationships.

The Contribution of Husbands and Wives to Family Incomes

We noted in the previous section that an increasing number of couples form dual earner housholds over a growing proportion of their working lives. Nonetheless it is still more likely that in terms of earnings the husband will make the major contribution to family income. The 1984 Family Expenditure Survey (FES) for example shows that married women contribute 23% of all income from employment in households where there are dependent children, and 32% where there are not, as shown in Figure 1.

Figure 1: Contribution of husbands' and wives' wages and salaries to family income

Non-retired households with married
women working, with dependent children
Average weekly income = £223.46

contribution of wife £52.11 (23.3%)
contribution of others £16.44 (7.4%)
contribution of head £154.91 (69.3%)

Married women working,
no dependent children
Average weekly income = £251.23

contribution of wife £81.97 (32.6%)
contribution of others £32.74 (13%)
contribution of head £136.52 (54.3%)

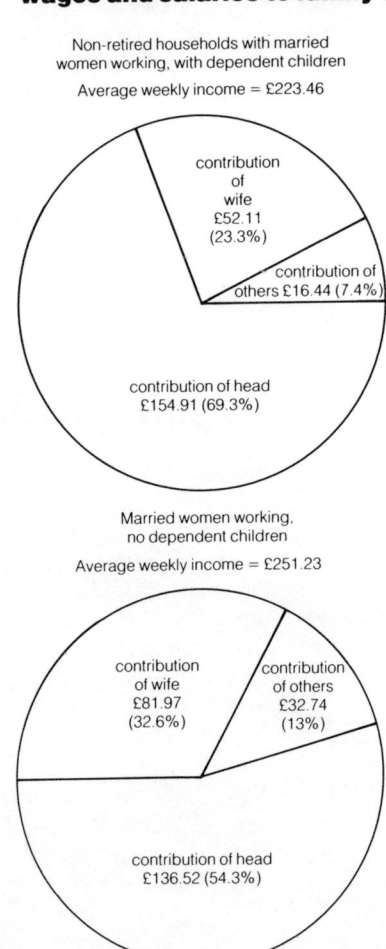

Source: Family Expenditure Survey 1984

This picture is borne out by the more detailed analysis of the FES for the years 1968, 1977 and 1980 by Elias (see Table 7 below). This showed that the proportion of employed wives with employed husbands who earned as much or more than their husbands had risen from 3.6% in 1968 to 8% in 1977 remaining at this level in 1980. If the analysis is limited to full time workers in both cases then the increase was from 5% (or 1 in 20) to 14.5% by 1977 (or 1 in 7), remaining stable at that level between 1977 and 1980.

This picture however needs to be interpreted cautiously in the light of the employment patterns described in Section Three. For example Table 7 shows that full time employee wives aged over 50 were most likely to earn as much or more than their husbands at both dates, and that wives with young children in the household are much less likely to do so.

Table 7: The proportion of wives earning as much or more than their husbands

Family/Employment Status	1968	1977
All employee wives with employee husbands (a)	3.6	8.0
Full time employee wives with full time employee husbands (b)	5.0	14.5
Case (a)		
Wives aged 20-34	2.7	9.3
Wives aged 35-49	3.3	5.2
Wives aged 50 and over	5.3	10.4
Case (b)		
Wives aged 20-34	3.4	15.9
Wives aged 35-49	5.8	10.4
Wives aged 50 and over	6.8	19.5
Case (a) Wives		
Children 0-1 present in household	0	5.1
Children 2-4 present in household	2.9	3.1
Children 5-16/18 present in household	2.0	3.7

Source: P. Elias, *The Changing Pattern of Employment and Earnings Among Married Couples 1968-1980.*

Tables 5, 6, and 7: *Equal Opportunities Commission Research Bulletin No.8.*

Other evidence also demonstrates that in the majority of couples the husbands' earnings exceed those of their wives. Marsh's survey of shift work, for example, showed that when a crude comparison was made between the take-home pay of husbands and wives in his sample, both of whom worked full time, there was a significant discrepancy in their earnings. The men did not simply earn more than the women, they earned nearly twice as much. Whereas the men's median income was around £48 per week (in 1977) the women's was around £27.[3] Only about 10% of women had incomes that exceeded those of their husbands, and many of these were wives of unemployed men. The majority of husbands earned over £15 per week more than their wives, and a quarter of them earned over £27 a week more.

More recently the Women and Employment Survey included an analysis of a sub-sample of couples. At the level of individual couples, working wives earned on average only about half of what their husbands earned. Only 7% of wives earned the same or more than their husbands. This was partly due to the women's shorter hours of work, but even on the basis of hourly earnings, wives' earnings were only 75% of those of their husbands.

However, the hourly earnings of wives who worked full time were 79% of their husbands' compared with 71% for women working part time. Only 15% of wives had the same as, or higher hourly earnings than their husbands and even among those working full time who generally have higher pay than part timers, only 20% had the same or higher hourly earnings than their husbands.[4]

The differential in men's and women's earnings is due to many factors. It can reflect differential qualifications and men's employment in occupations with higher pay. Equally the effects of family formation (and subsequent part time work and frequent downward occupational mobility) have been shown to depress women's lifetime earnings.

For individual couples these patterns vary, of course, not only with age and stage of family building, but also with the educational level of the partners. It might be expected that the rise in the educational attainment of females in recent years will lead to some improvement in the relative position of women in the labour market, although these inequalities are deeply entrenched and institutionalised.

Given this greater economic power of men, it might be

expected that they would have more control over the way in which resources are allocated between couples. For evidence on this we turn to consider patterns of money management within marriage.

Money Management and Resource Control

"One basic consideration of the distribution of financial power within marriage is that for most women it is so obviously unequal that it does not need mentioning." [5]

There is growing research evidence that some separated and divorced women find themselves financially better off than they were during marriage. This throws light on the area of money management between husband and wife. A central conclusion to be drawn is, as Hilary Graham observes:

"It is not only the economic position of the family that shapes a woman's standard of living in marriage, it is also the distribution of the family's material resources among and between parents and children." [6]

Much work on this distribution of money within households has followed a classificatory typology developed by Jan Pahl.[7]

1. The whole wage system, in which one partner, usually the wife, is responsible for managing all the household finances, except possibly the personal spending money of the other partner. This system is typically associated with low incomes.

2. The allowance system, in which typically the husband gives his wife a set amount of money and she is responsible for some expenditure such as for housekeeping, while the rest of the money remains in his control and he pays for other items.

3. The pooling system, in which both partners have access to all the household money and both are responsible for managing the common pool and for expenditure. Pooling or jointness is more likely to occur as income rises, and when the wife is in employment.

4. The independent management system, in which both partners have an income which they maintain separately, neither having access to all the financial resources of the household. In this system each partner is responsible for specific items of expenditure; these responsibilities may change over time but the principle of keeping flows of money separate within the household is maintained.

Pahl's evidence suggests that the allowance system and the independent management system are the ones in which husbands would not necessarily transfer additional money in their pay packet — such as might result from overtime or changes in tax allowances or family credit — to the wife or to the family, and it is therefore important in policy terms to know how extensive each pattern is, and what factors influence this.

Table 8 below shows the proportion of couples in each category, drawing evidence from Pahl's study in Kent[8] and from a national postal survey carried out at the University of Surrey.[9] Both surveys found that just under a quarter of husbands give their wives an allowance, retaining the rest of their earnings; over half use a pooling system; and the remaining quarter use either the whole wage or the independent management system.

Table 8: Frequency of four types of allocative system

	Pahl Study (Kent 1982-83)	University of Surrey Study (Britain 1983)
Whole wage system	14	18
Allowance system	22	24
Pooling system	56	54
Independent management system	9	4
Total	**100**	**100**
Number	**102**	**250**

Source: J. Pahl, *Taxation and Family Financial Management*, July 1985.

Evidence from the two studies quoted above suggests that the allowance system is typically found among higher income households where either the husband is the only earner or he earns much more than his wife. This is shown in Table 9.

Table 9: How couples' system of money management relates to income

annual household income (take-home pay)	whole wage	allowance system	pooling system	independent system	all
	%	%	%	%	%
up to £9,000 pa	93	36	63	33	59
£9,000+ pa	7	64	37	67	41

Source: J. Pahl, *Taxation and Family Financial Management*, 1985

In both the independent management system and the allowance system, wives will not necessarily know what their husbands earn. A survey by the Occupational Pensions Board suggested that half of all wives did not know their husband's earnings.[10] More recent evidence from Marsh's survey shows that only two thirds of the wives could give a figure for their husband's earnings,[11] which is consistent with evidence from the Women and Employment Survey. When this was compared with the figures the husbands gave as their earnings — and assuming this figure was a reliable one — 15% of wives over-estimated their husband's income, 43% of them got it right, 24% thought it up to £9 per week less than the sum reported by the husband, and a significant 16% thought it more than £9 less than the real figure. Part of the explanation of the divergence between wives' views of husbands' income and true income may be due to fluctuations in overtime payments which the wife may not know about, and which the husband may regard as discretionary income.

In general, systems of money management adopted by couples will reflect the relative importance of a number of key variables. i.e:

- income level of the couple
- source of income
- employment pattern
- lifecycle stage

As Table 9 indicates, when income is low the whole wage or pooling systems are more likely. An allowance arrangement is more likely as income rises. Pooling and independent money management are both generally more likely where both partners are employed; conversely an allowance system is most likely where the husband is the sole earner.

Other studies, such as those of Wilson[12] and Brannen and Moss[13] reveal how women underplay their role in family finances. Wilson's study also confirms the importance of income level and sources of income affecting the pattern of management adopted. In her study the management of resources in low income households fell to one person in 18 out of 24 households. Of these only one was a man.

As income rose the likelihood of having 2 earners increased, and one person took financial responsibility in only 9 out of 22 cases (again only one was the man). Equally, the fact that there are two earners means that women are more likely to shoulder financial responsibilities than in single earner households.

At higher income levels all the women who earned had their own bank account and paid at least one bill. Wilson identified two very distinct patterns in households with working wives. Either these women were solely responsible for all aspects of family consumption and able to finance their activities largely from their own earnings, or they managed their own money and had the potential to share in financial decisions.

On the other hand, women who did not earn had relatively little financial responsibility. While they might actually pay the bills they knew little about family finances and "left all that to their husbands".

The incidence of a whole wage system under female control seems to be associated with a rigid division of labour between the sexes. Some research has suggested that this is confirmed by the prevalence of the system in the north of England. However, its occurrence also in the East Midlands, Wales and the south west may indicate that other cultural variables are significant.[14]

There is some evidence of change over time: younger households are generally more likely to use pooling or independent money management than are their parents. As Morris and Ruane comment:

"(this) . . . may be associated with changing ideas about gender roles and the nature of marriage, as Pahl suggests. But it may also reflect other changes, such as improved levels of income for many, and increased labour market participation by married women. If this is the case, then we should expect other changes to follow as a result of recession and social polarisation." [15]

Management and Control

Patterns of domestic money management are interesting since they relate to broader questions of gender roles and of power. It is likely that there is an association between patterns of housekeeping and gender role relationships. Elizabeth Bott, for example, has suggested that inflexible housekeeping arrangements parallel highly segregated role relationships, while flexible financial arrangements match more joint role relationships.[16]

Whether the system of financial management is a *reflection* of power within a relationship, or its *source*, is an obvious area of interest. It is likely that in fact the pattern is circular or mutually reinforcing. Much of the research evidence on spending patterns has identified these as complementary to traditional gender roles. One characteristically female spending pattern, for example, has been labelled 'maternal altruism'. That is, a pattern in which the needs of the family and children are always treated as paramount, and come before those of the wife and mother. The male pattern, on the other hand, is very often one much more concerned with personal spending power.

"Indeed it would seem that gender attitudes towards spending have grown out of the traditional sexual division of labour. In this context, writers have commented that constraints in women's spending derive not simply from access to money, but also from the view that they have no right to what they have not 'earned' in the formal and narrowly defined sense implied by paid employment." [17]

Similar work to that of Pahl has been carried out by Meredith Edwards in Australia.[18] Both studies draw the important distinction between the **'management'** and **'control'** aspects of family finances. While the manager handles family money, they may not have a role in financial decision making — the control function. Indeed Edwards suggests that one of the most significant findings in financial management is the prevalence of systems in which wives *manage* family finances, combined with the small number of wives who could be said to have overall *control* of the finances.

These dimensions of control and management are apparently recognised by couples. Graham reports that disagreements over money typically feature criticism of men's *control* of money while wives are accused of *mismanagement*. Some of the comments made by the women in her survey indicate that even more than this the disagreements are over who should *benefit* from expenditure. A couple of examples make the point:

"Ronald didn't like me buying anything for the children. If I went out and bought them a pair of shoes and he wasn't with me, there was hell to pay when I got home. He just didn't like me spending money without his consent. If he wanted to go out and buy things that was different. He was very keen on photography and he bought a lot of photographic equipment. What things he wanted to buy was OK, but the basics and things I needed to get for the children, he thought were unreasonable."

"His hobby is fishing and do-it-yourself things and he'll just go and buy the tools and I think 'Oh that money, what I could have bought with that money'. So I will budget and go around the markets and that, and find the best buys and he'll just go to the best shops because it is convenient." [19]

The issue of control of money is so important that many women in Graham's research who — objecively — were poorer as lone parents actually felt much better off:

"I'm better off I think. Although I have less money, it's all mine to allocate where I want. It's made a difference to how I organise money because I have control now."

Similarly,

"I'm worse off overall. I probably have less money (. . . .) But I feel as though I'm better off." [20]

The management and control dichotomy is evident in other aspects of intra-household resource distribution. We have seen in earlier sections that the domestic domain is primarily a female one. It may be surprising therefore that while women generally have major responsibility for food preparation they may not have control over its nature. Graham's research with lone mothers found 74% reporting a change in their diet, with a move away from their ex-partner's food preferences. In part this reflects self-determination, although for many women it was also a deliberate coping strategy in dealing with poverty and lone motherhood by choosing cheaper food.

Other research, however, also indicates that inequalities in the distribution of financial and other resources in households are reflected and reinforced at the dining table. As Millar and Glendinning have pointed out, most studies of poverty "have largely focused on the financial circumstances of families or household units. They therefore fail to recognise the extent of the poverty which is experienced by women, and the particular dimensions and causes of that poverty."[21] Just so with research on eating habits. Charles and Kerr criticise the methodology of research on food consumption which simply divides the amount of food entering a household by the number of members. Their own research into families from a wide range of social backgrounds produces clear evidence of inequalities. Women generally subordinate their own food *preferences* to those of partners and children, there are also disparities in food *consumption* — particularly of 'higher status' foods:

"Food is not a resource to which all family members have equal access (. . .) Thus men consume high status food and drink more frequently than do women and children (. . .) These inequalities are more marked in some families than others but they nevertheless appear to typify all families at this life cycle point when most women and children are financially dependent on men. The consumption of food therefore conveys messages about the status of those that consume it and depends upon relations of power between family members, with the most powerful consuming the most and the best." [22]

As Graham has also suggested, Charles and Kerr argue that women's control over food shopping and cooking "does not necessarily lead to their wielding power in their own interests" — rather these are subordinate to the interests of partners and children. The sexual division of labour evident in the home, the divisions around the management and control of financial resources, are reflected in and reproduced by even the pattern of food distribution in households.

Control and Independent Income

Edwards' work also showed that the amount of money which a husband allocated his wife for housekeeping did not automatically rise in line with either prices or husbands' income. In the UK discussion of this issue arose first in the early 1970s as part of the consideration of the impact of inflation on household budgets. At that time a PEP Survey on inflation, for example, showed that although people in general assumed that housewives as a group — and the wives of semi-skilled and unskilled manual workers in particular — would suffer particularly acutely from inflation this was not the case if the proportionate rise in housekeeping was compared with the proportionate rise in men's earnings. The percentage rise in housekeeping was in fact *greater* than that for net earnings for all social classes. However, those on the lowest household budgets — in this case social classes C1 and D — waited longer periods between housekeeping increases and there was a high level of dissatisfaction in the group who had had their housekeeping increased in the most distant past.[23] Similar evidence of a lag in uprating housekeeping was provided in a study of Bethnal Green, where 48% of women were affected.[24]

More recently the debate has returned to the role of state benefits for children as a source of independent income for mothers.[25] And Edwards' survey, for example showed that for those women lacking paid employment (usually those with pre-school aged children), or with little say over financial control, family allowances were an important independent source of income. Similarly, a survey by CPAG in 1985 documented the importance of child benefit both to middle class and working class mothers — to those on reasonable as well as low incomes — child benefit was often crucial in 'making ends meet', and generally in providing for the day to day needs of children which typically fell to the mother.[26]

Unemployment and Money Management

It is clear that systems of money management are not immutable. They can change for example when the woman gives up work, when the nature of dependency changes, such as the arrival of an elderly relative, or when young people start working. It is also important and interesting to look at evidence on patterns in families affected by unemployment.

A follow-up study of a sub-sample of unemployed women in the OPCS Women and Employment Survey, for example, showed different patterns to those outlined above for families in work.[27] In about 17% of the married couples the wife had sole control over the household economy, to the extent of determining the amount of 'pocket money' available to the husband. In about a quarter of households, mainly those with higher incomes and those where the wife worked, financial control was shared, sometimes involving joint bank accounts. However the most common practice was for the wife to receive a housekeeping allowance with most cases falling in the £40-£60 per week range (1980/81 prices).

This study served to highlight the tensions which could arise in some systems of financial management, when income had fallen from a previously higher level. This was particularly the case with the allowance system, partly due to the "dependent, supplicatory role in which the wife was placed". But it also reflected the husband's failure to understand the cost of routine purchases, and the desire of the wife to have some money to spend on herself.

Since the follow up study was conducted seven to nine months after the major Women and Employment Survey, it provided some insight into the way management systems and levels of allowance *change* when wives re-enter employment. It was significant that among the couples with both partners in work at the time of the later Survey, not only were the husband's earnings invariably higher than the wife's, but in about half the cases, mainly where the wife worked part time and with low earnings, she still received the same amount of housekeeping as she had prior to finding work. Her own earnings were regarded as an extra entirely for her own use. Among the remaining couples however there was some suggestion that the wife's revived earning power encouraged joint financial control over both incomes.

It is clear that as well as there being disagreements over the amount of allowances, there may often be some tensions about the ownership of income from the husband's earnings:

"At bottom, most of the women with the housekeeping allowance, together with some of the others, regarded the husband's income as his to dispose of as he saw fit, on the grounds that he earned it, rather than as a genuinely joint resource." [28]

This was the case even when the husband regarded his earnings as a joint resource:

"He regards it (husband's wage) as ours. I regard it as his. I never look at his wage slip or ask him how much he has earned. He gives me the housekeeping and takes care of the bills. If I run short I just ask for more and he tells me to help myself. I feel though that it is his money because I am not contributing any more." [29]

Women's Earnings

A major explanation which married women often offer for seeking work is their desire for an independent income. It might be expected that the increased economic activity of women would therefore lead to greater independence in household money management. However, rather than providing personal spending money, the evidence is that married women overwhelmingly use their earnings to augment the housekeeping. 'Extra' money which men can earn (such as from overtime), on the other hand, is often used as a personal resource (however, much of the research findings in this area are now fairly dated and the role of overtime may well be different under changed economic circumstances). Morris and Ruane point out that while an independent income for women may indeed decrease the control of the male breadwinner, this is *not* the same as increased jointness in financial management and control.

The proportion of their own income women spend on housekeeping is fairly high across all social classes although it tends to fall as social class rises. Thus wives of unskilled manual workers may use some 69% of their own earnings for the family compared with 50% of those married to managerial/professional workers.

"Effects will vary with the nature of the job, levels of pay, its associated status, whether there is any challenge to other aspects of the division of labour within the home, what cultural factors are strong in the particular locality etc." [30]

It might be further expected that the (generally) greater power of men within the family reflects their major contribution to household income. Clearly this is an over-simplification and relates to the earlier point that financial management patterns reflect and reinforce existing gender divisions. Households in which women make a greater financial contribution, do not necessarily reveal reversed money management systems.

Peggy Stamp, for example, examined financial arrangements in households in which the *female* was the main earner. The incidence of joint or independent money management was lower (44%) than might have been anticipated. Moreover, the allowance system so familiar to housewives was totally unknown to these males.

"The indications are then that an income for women is not sufficient entirely to overcome issues of gender identity and gender roles in the management of household finances." [31]

Banking Arrangements

The banking arrangements for couples, that is whether they have only sole accounts, only joint, or a combination of these, also varies. The previous discussion of household financial management systems is consistent with findings that joint bank accounts are least likely at lower occupational levels. Social class C2 are most likely to have only joint accounts, while groups A and AB are more likely to have a variety of arrangements.

Trends in banking services in recent times mean that a bank account can be much more than simply somewhere to keep cash. Morris and Ruane point to the increase of transfer payments. In 1976 only one quarter of regular household commitments were managed by authorised payments (standing order, and direct debit etc). This had risen to one third in 1981 and to 40% by 1985. What might the implications of this be? Morris and Ruane suggest the following:

"(. . .) given married women's concentration in part time low paid employment with a greater probability of cash payment, an increase in transfer payments may increase male involvement in household expenditure. We have already noted a tendency for this form of payment to encourage male payments of large, regular outgoings, and the rise in pre-authorised payment seems consistent with this. Correspondingly, there will be a growing dependence of non-working women on male decisions about spending, and possibly an increased incentive for them to seek employment." [32]

Another trend has been the great increase in the use of plastic cards, particularly of cash dispenser cards. As

Morris and Ruane again remark, these too may pose a "challenge to mutually agreed systems of finance management, presenting the potential for more individual access and decision making."[33]

The Ownership of Property Within Marriage

The management and control of family *income* is not the only measure of financial power. The question of 'resources' more broadly defined — including assets and ownership of major goods and property — is too large to be dealt with adequately here. However, one area of particular interest is that of home ownership. With an increasing trend towards owner occupation, whether the husband, wife or both are registered as owners of the marital home is of growing importance.

The 1983 General Household Survey found that 38% of house owners (i.e owned on a mortgage or outright) had their home registered in the name of the head of household only. 55% however had joint ownership between wife and head of household. It might be expected that this is an increasing trend. Certainly it is most common among younger couples.

Cohabitation and Financial Arrangements

While our concern so far as been with married couples, the financial relationships of cohabiting couples are also of interest and have been studied as part of the administration of Supplementary Benefit (the SB rules assume that in cohabiting couples the woman is financially supported by her partner).

An official report on cohabitation in 1971 included a question on whether there was a pooled household fund in a 'combination of facts' approach to defining whether or not couples were cohabiting. Part of the evidence on the working of the cohabitation rule was a study by Ruth Lister on fifty cases of alleged cohabitation.[34] In only 4 out of 49 cases where financial questions were answered did the alleged cohabitee make any real financial contribution to the support of the household. In 8 more cases a limited contribution was made, usually for meals consumed, and in addition, 7 men were paying for the maintenance of their child. Again, only 4 out of 49 said that they pooled their resources.

This study identified as problematic the case in which the cohabitee was not the father of some of the woman's children. Lister suggested that the men were mostly willing to contribute to their own, and their own children's keep, but they did not feel responsible for any other children the women might have. An administrative change was subsequently introduced to provide for discretionary payments for the first four weeks after benefit was withdrawn, of the amount included in the supplementary allowance for any children of whom the man was not the father. Even these changes did not appear to have overcome the major problems with the cohabitation rule and it was noted that women frequently claimed benefit again after it had been withdrawn on the grounds of cohabitation.

The situation of cohabitation amongst previously married couples and the financial support of children from a previous marriage is likely to become more common with increasing levels of divorce and remarriage, on which a major new survey will throw light.[35] Studies of divorced and remarried couples may well prove a useful source of information on financial arrangements.

This section has mainly considered the evidence on the management and control of household incomes between husbands and wives. The different allocation systems identified by Pahl and others have been analysed. We have seen that the *actual* allocation system adopted by couples will be influenced by a number of variables including: socio-economic position; source of income; men's and women's employment; stage of life-cycle, and social and cultural norms and traditions. It may be seen that many women have little control over household income, and little knowledge of their partner's income. By and large these patterns are related to broader features of gender roles and segregation between men and women.

We have also pointed out, however, that very much more remains to be known about the actual processes affecting couples' financial arrangements. In particular, the impact of unemployment, of more sophisticated banking and credit facilities, and changes over time (both within households and inter-generationally) would all be fruitful areas for further research and analysis.

Summary:
Inside the Family: An Overview
Melanie Henwood

In this paper we have reviewed evidence on the changing roles of men and women within the family. The family today reflects dimensions of both change and continuities. The changes are perhaps more evident, and the subject of much of the debate over the 'future of the family'. The increase in married women's employment is arguably one of the most dramatic post-war developments, and has seen the rise of the dual worker/dual career family. For the individuals such changes present new challenges and opportunities, as well as generating new dilemmas and problems. For most households it is still true that any ideological commitment to equality usually bows — to a lesser or greater extent — to operational and financial pragmatism.

A picture of inequality can, however, be viewed from two sides. The diagram below illustrates some major responsibilities of men and women inside and outside the home. A number of features can be highlighted.

- The home domain is still very much a female one. Women are still primarily responsible for domestic and caring tasks, although 50% couples claim to share child care equally.

- While women are mainly or solely responsible for almost three quarters of all housework, men are primarily responsible for over 80% of household repairs.

- While women have become increasingly active in the labour market, for many this is still largely secondary to their roles as wives and mothers — most married women with children who work do so part time.

- Men spend less time at home, but generally work longer hours in their jobs. Even women employed full time rarely work as many hours as their male colleagues.

● Female employees (both full and part time) generally have less free time at home than males. While spending fewer hours at work (or travelling to and from work) they spend much longer on domestic work, shopping etc: while full time male employees have around 10.2 hours of free time per weekend day, and 2.6 during the week, for full time female employees the respective figures are 7.2 hours and 2.1 hours.

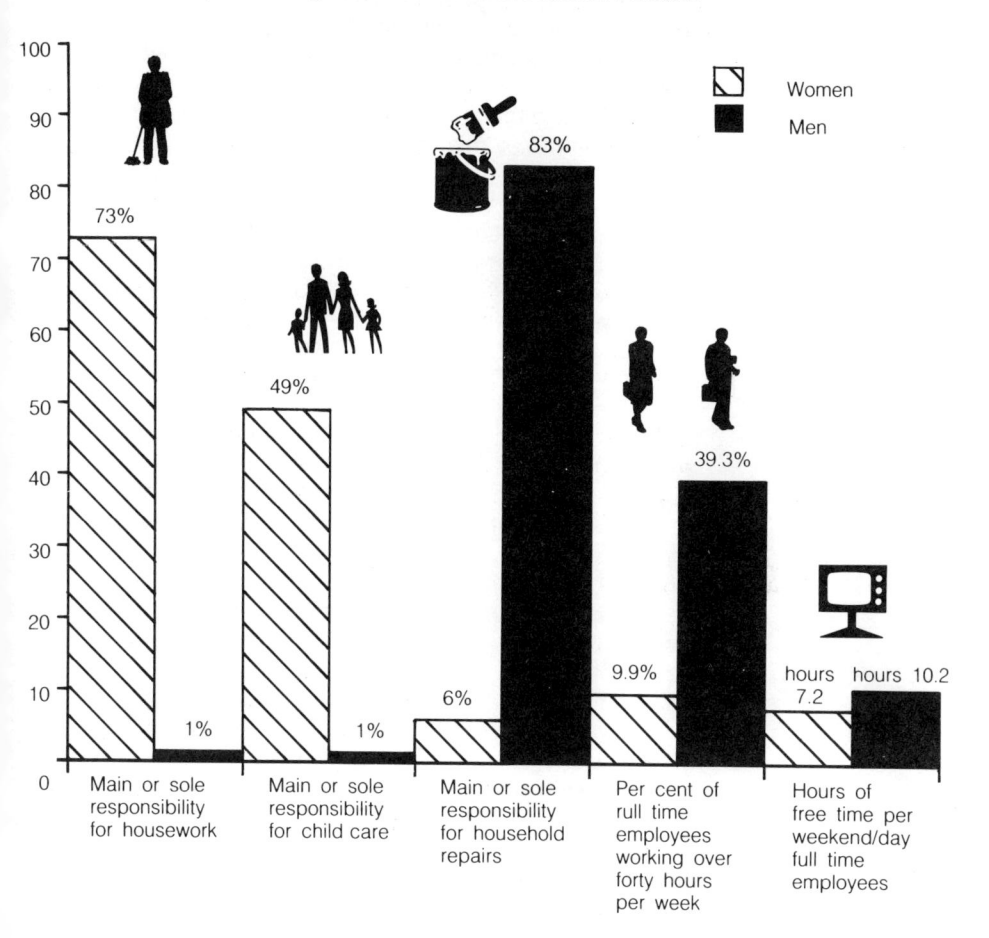

Women
Men

Category	Women	Men
Main or sole responsibility for housework	73%	1%
Main or sole responsibility for child care	49%	1%
Main or sole responsibility for household repairs	6%	83%
Per cent of full time employees working over forty hours per week	9.9%	39.3%
Hours of free time per weekend/day full time employees	7.2 hours	10.2 hours

Sources: Dept of Employment /OPCS, *Women and Employment* HMSO 1984
R Jowell & S Witherspoon (eds) *British Social Attitudes, the 1985 Report* Gower 1985
CSO, *Social Trends 17*, HMSO 1987

Note: Diagram only shows *main* responsibilities for domestic work and child care, it does not indicate where such tasks are shared and percentages do not therefore add up to 100.

Section 5: Private Families and Public Policy

Malcolm Wicks

What occurs inside the family may well be of public interest, but surely it is not a matter for public *policy*? Indeed should not government steer well clear of the private world of the family? How men and women order their own lives is their business, not that of bureaucrats and politicians. Yet, this seemingly sensible stricture is less helpful in the real world. Government *is* involved with insider family dealing, nor would it be easily otherwise, given the scope of social politics in modern societies. Policies, practices, and procedures about such matters as employment, taxation, social security and child care raise important questions — and often demand judgements — that impinge on internal family dynamics — for good or ill.

This is no recent development, as a glance back at the pages of our social history testifies. Politicians and officials have made judgements in the past about the internal domain of the family and who should get what within it. When national health insurance was first introduced, for example, government actuaries explained the exclusion of married women in the following way:

"Married women living with their husbands need not be included since where the unit is the family, it is the husband's and not the wife's health which it is important to insure. So long as the husband is in good health, and able to work adequate provision will be made for the needs of the family, irrespective of the wife's health, whereas when the husband's health fails there is no one to earn wages." [1]

Similarly, William Beveridge in his 1942 Report made some clear assumptions about the respective roles and rights of men and women within the family which underpinned his detailed social security plans.

". . . all women by marriage acquire a new economic and social status, with risks and rights different from those of the unmarried. On marriage a woman gains a legal right

to maintenance by her husband as a first line of defence against risks which fall directly on the solitary woman; she undertakes at the same time to perform vital unpaid service . . ." [2]

Furthermore:

"Every woman on marriage will become a new person, acquiring new rights and not carrying on into marriage claims to unemployment or disability benefit in respect of contributions made before marriage." [3]

Social Security

Since Beveridge's time questions concerning the relationship between men and women within the family have remained on the agenda. This is certainly true within the field of family finances. There have been some particularly lively debates concerning child support. The early advocates of family allowances, including Eleanor Rathbone and the Family Endowment Society, were absolutely clear that allowances should be paid to the mother. As one commentator notes:

"It would help rectify the situation in which motherhood was 'generally regarded not as a service necessary to the community but as a service to an individual man, a private luxury on which he may or may not choose to spend his surplus income', and would guarantee that the money would be wisely spent on the children." [4]

This proposal was readily accepted by the legislators of the 1940s but has not gone unchallenged in the years since then. For example, under the Child Benefit Bill of 1975 family allowances and child tax allowances were to be replaced by a unified child benefit: a tax-free, flat rate sum paid to mothers in respect of every dependent child up to 16. Much was made of the supposed transfer from 'wallet to purse', and the recognition of the important role of mothers. The then Social Services Secretary, Barbara Castle, commented that the wife and mother "certainly needs control of her own budget if the family is to be fed and clothed". However the new Child Benefit scheme was almost strangled at birth because of alarm over the very 'wallet to purse' transfer. Some members of the Cabinet became anxious lest the adverse impact on men's wage-packets of phasing out child tax allowances might jeopardise wage restraint. A behind the scenes deal was done to end the scheme and it was only the outcry following a leak of Cabinet papers that saved the initiative and hence the child benefit for mothers.[5]

More recently the proposal, following the Social Security Reviews, to transform Family Income Supplement into a new Family Credit scheme ran into similarly controversial waters. The Government proposed that the new Family Credit should be paid through wage packets and therefore, within families, mainly to men. Despite much outcry, from a wide range of sources, the Government stuck doggedly to the proposal throughout all but the remaining stage of the parliamentary process. Then, at the eleventh hour, the Government announced a change of heart and the Family Credit will now go to mothers.

Family Taxation

Focusing on issues inside the family lays bare the traditional policy assumption that government only has to provide benefits for the family in order to ensure that needs are catered for adequately. Evidence about family dynamics, internal income distribution and expenditure patterns have challenged this assumption and today there is growing interest in what is the appropriate unit for social policy assessment and entitlement purposes.

"In theory, there are a number of possible options for the tax and benefit unit:
● *the individual (as in national insurance contributions);*
● *the (married) couple (as in the UK tax system);*
● *the family (as in the French tax system — 'quotient familiale');*
● *the household (as in the national assistance system in the 1930s)."* [6]

The existing system in Britain is, as one commentator has observed, "a complex amalgam of several of these units, one that has grown up piecemeal over a number of years".[7]

In recent times it has been family taxation that has provoked the most lively discussion, not least because of the Government's own interest as witnessed by two Green Papers.[8] Generally a woman's income chargeable to tax is treated as the income of her husband and aggregated with his. This has been the case since the start of the Income Tax System in 1799. Today the future of the married man's tax allowance, with all its implication of wives' dependency, prompts particular debate.

The issue also occurs within social security where, for example, it is assumed that an out of work married person is being supported by his/her spouse and therefore not normally entitled to supplementary benefits. There has been particular controversy about cohabiting couples. The issues are controversial because crucial questions of values, as well as policy, are involved. Should an individual's status as regards taxation and benefits change on marriage or not? The upholders of traditional family values and feminists will obviously take different lines on this one. As has been noted:

". . . the basic conflict is between the desire to treat individuals equitably, and 'in their own right', and at the same time to recognise the role and structure of households and their effect on an individual's standard of living." [9]

Family Care

The care of elderly people, and other dependent groups too, raises important questions about sex equality. Most family care is provided by women, often the daughters or daughters-in-law of those being cared for. Many women have to leave employment in order to provide such care. While the historical trend towards smaller families has been a liberating one for women, enabling them to spend relatively less of their lives providing care to children, the ageing of the population now threatens this freedom, bringing as it does huge demands for care at the other end of the life cycle. How can these increasing needs be tackled without affecting women adversely is one of the most vital — and difficult — questions in contemporary social policy. And, while changes in attitudes are crucial if men and women are to share care in the future, the right kind of social policy infrastructure is also essential.[10]

Some of the most obvious — and pressing — matters concern the front-line provision of health and social services. Adequate support for carers is important rather than it being assumed that the existence of a (normally female) carer somehow absolves the state from responsibility. A partnership between family and the state is required here, but the community care policy agenda does not end with these services.

One recent controversy illustrates the policy debate. Until recently the Invalid Care Allowance was restricted in its scope. It applied initially to carers who were close relatives, and later covered anyone caring for a disabled person in receipt of Attendance Allowance, *with the sole exclusion of married (and cohabiting) women.* A test case went before the European Court. On the eve of a judgement from the Court which would have compelled Britain to cease the discriminatory provisions of the Invalid Care Allowance, the Government announced that ICA would, after all, be extended to the estimated 70,000 women previously excluded. The arguments over ICA were of long standing. The case for extending entitlement to married and cohabiting women (rather than restricting it to *single* women and *men of any marital status*) had long been resisted. It had been said that the cost would be too great. Implicit at least was the assumption on the part of successive governments that women were 'natural' carers, and that married women were at home ready and willing to undertake such a role with no recompense or social security entitlement.

Dilemmas of Reform

The reform process is not one without its own dilemmas. Those who wish to redress unequal relationships between men and women within the family need to tread warily, lest new measures reinforce sex stereotyping. Given inequalities and the unequal burdens within the family it is sensible to ensure that help goes to those undertaking the work, mainly women. Hence all the important arguments about who should receive child benefit and other forms of family income support. Hence also the whole rise of interest in the subject of 'carers' and the need to ensure that those providing care are treated fairly. But by providing such help policy might encourage, certainly reinforce, the assumption that child rearing and more general family care is essentially women's work, albeit work that should be better regarded and supported in the future than in the recent past.

Another dilemma is illustrated by recent changes to divorce legislation. Under the Matrimonial and Family Proceedings Act 1984 the principle underlying the granting of maintenance has changed. The former requirement was to seek to place the parties following a divorce in the financial position in which they would have been if the marriage had not broken down. Now the guiding principle regarding the position of former wives (separate provision applies for children) places "greater emphasis on the desirability of the parties becoming self-sufficient so far as is possible, and empowers the courts to dismiss outright an application for maintenance payments".[11]

How should this change be viewed? In principle, it could be argued that it is a modern day provision, one that no longer views women as invariably financially dependent (on men) and thus recognises fully the force of contemporary female employment patterns. Nevertheless, critics repeatedly raised two issues during the parliamentary debates: the limited earnings capacity of women responsible for the care of young children and the longer term impact of family responsibilities during marriage on women's earnings potential in later years. What critics were really saying is that there is no point legislating away the concept of dependency if it exists in practice with the consequent danger of impoverishing women following marital breakdown.

Conclusion

There exists a tension between an infrastructure of policy and practice, much of it traditional in its assumptions about the roles, rights and responsibilities of men and women, and the rise of new, feminist, perspectives. Against the old assumptions there have developed counter pressures based on an analysis of the alleged, sexist nature of contemporary policy — the ways in which legislation is cast in a man's world and therefore clearly defines the woman's role as homemaker and child carer.

Partly because of this analysis, but more generally because of a stronger mainstream current of pressure in favour of women's rights, there has been a small, but not insignificant, stream of legislation and policy that has sought to redress the balance. In the employment field, for example, the Employment Protection Act and the Sex Discrimination Act bear testimony to change as does the Equal Opportunities Commission. For child care, to take another example, despite much criticism about the inadequacy of provision, there has been a growth of child care facilities.

Contemporary policy therefore has been influenced by a

mixture of principles, perspectives and prejudices. Some policies are based on traditional assumptions about male-female roles, others on quite different ones. The issues are controversial — more so today than, say, a decade ago. They are on the public agenda however. What happens inside the family is not just a private matter.

Appendix 1

Arrangement of hours and average hours worked per day by full and part time workers on a typical working day. (Martin and Roberts: *Women and Employment* Op Cit. Table 4.7)

Arrangement of Hours

Mornings	Starting before 10am Finishing before 2pm
Short day (am)	Starting before 10am Finishing 2pm or later, but before 4pm
Standard day	Starting before 10am Finishing 4pm or later but before 6pm
Long day	Starting before 10am Finishing 6pm or later
Mid-day	Starting 10am or later Finishing before 4pm
Short day (pm)	Starting 10am or later Finishing 4pm or later but before 6pm
Late day	Starting 10am or later Finishing 6pm or later
Evenings	Starting 4pm or later Finishing before midnight
Nights	Starting 4pm or later Finishing midnight or later

References

Introduction

1 Ronald Fletcher: *The Family and Marriage in Britain* Third Edition Pelican 1973

2 Ibid, p9

3 'Britons Observed' *The Observer* colour supplement, October 1984

4 Roger Jowell & Colin Airey (eds) *British Social Attitudes* (1984) Gower

5 Patrick West: 'The Family, the Welfare State and Community Care: Political rhetoric and public attitudes'. *Journal of Social Policy* Vol 13, Part 4 October 1984 pp417-446

6 'They're all in the family' editorial *The Guardian* 6.6.86

7 David Owen: *A United Kingdom* (1986) Penguin p183

8 B Thorne: 'Feminist rethinking of the family: An overview' in Thorne, B and Yalom, M (eds) *Rethinking the Family* (1982) Longmans p1

9 CSO *Social Trends 17* Table 2.1 HMSO 1987

10 Mike Murphy: *The Life Course of Individuals in the Family*, OPCS/British Society for Population Studies, Occasional Paper 21, OPCS 1983

11 M Young & P Willmott: *The Symmetrical Family* (1973) Routledge and Kegan Paul

12 Ibid p29

13 Ibid p30

14 Ibid p32

15 Charlie Lewis and Margaret O'Brien (eds): *Reassessing Fatherhood*, 1987. Sage p1

16 John Cunningham: 'Macho may be the role image, but is a new man emerging?' *The Guardian* 20.2.85

17 Caroline St John Brooks: 'The truce between men and women' *New Society* 3.1.85

Section 1 The Family and the Home

1   Caroline St John Brooks 1985, op cit

2   J Martin and C Roberts: *Women and Employment*: A lifetime perspective. DE/OPCS, 1984 London HMSO

3   Ann Oakley: *The Sociology of Housework* (1974) Basil Blackwell, 1985

4   Elizabeth Bott: *Family and Social Network*, Tavistock 1957

5   Oakley, 1974 op cit p162

6   R Jowell & S Witherspoon (eds) *British Social Attitudes*. The 1985 Report. Gower, 1985 p56

7   Martin & Roberts 1984, op cit

8   Ibid

9   Ibid

10   Ibid p100

11   C Airey & R Jowell, 1984. Op cit p133

12   Jowell & Witherspoon, 1985. Op cit

13   Julia Brannen & Peter Moss: 'Fathers in dual-earner households — through mothers' eyes' in C Lewis and M O'Brien (eds) 1987. Op cit p134

14   Airey & Jowell, 1984, op cit p134

15   Ibid

16   Ibid p133

17   'Britons Obvserved' reported in *The Observer* colour supplement, 16.9.84

18   M Young & P Willmott, 1973. Op cit p31

19   Young & Willmott op cit p93

20   Young & Willmott op cit p278

21   Ann Oakley op cit p164

22   Brannen & Moss 1987 op cit

23   Ibid p135

24   Oakley, 1974, op cit p165

Section 2　Family Care

1　Lesley Rimmer, 'The Economics of Work and Caring', in Janet Finch and Dulcie Groves (eds), *A Labour of Love*, Routledge and Kegan Paul, 1983

2　Hilary Graham, 'Caring: A Labour of Love', in Finch & Groves, op cit, p18

3　Barrie Thorne, 'Feminist Rethinking of the Family: an overview', in Barrie Thorne and Marilyn Yalom (eds), *Rethinking the Family*, Longman, 1982 p11

4　Libby Purves: 'Searching for the new fatherland' *The Times* 8.9.86

5　Ibid

6　Charlie Lewis and Margaret O'Brien (eds) *Reassessing Fatherhood*, Sage 1987

7　R. Jowell & S. Witherspoon (eds) *British Social Attitudes*, the 1985 Report, Gower 1985

8　David Piachaud: *Round about fifty hours a week*, CPAG 1984

9　Ibid p10

10　Ibid p14

11　Ibid p19

12　Ibid p18

13　J. Martin & C. Roberts: *Women and Employment*. A lifetime perspective. Department of Employment/OPCS. HMSO 1984 p102

14　Ann Oakley 1974 op cit

15　Ibid p155

16　Britons Observed, *The Observer* Colour Supplement, October 1984

17　Lewis and O'Brien 1987 op cit p3

18　Ibid p4

19　Piachaud 1984 op cit p22

20　C Bell; L McKee; K Priestly: *Fathers, Childbirth and Work*, Equal Opportunities Commission, 1983 p9

21　Lewis and O'Brien, 1987, op cit p5

22　Peter Moss & Julia Brannen 'Fathers and employment' in Lewis and O'Brien, 1987, op cit

23　Ibid

24　Piachaud 1984 op cit p22

25 Jo Roll: *Babies and Money: birth trends and costs.* Occasional Paper No 4 FPSC, 1986

26 Piachaud 1984 op cit p22

27 Gillian Parker: *With Due Care & Attention: a review of research on informal care.* Occasional Paper No 2. FPSC 1985

28 *An Ageing Population* Fact Sheet 2 Family Policy Studies Centre 1986

29 DHSS: *Growing Older.* Cmnd 8173, 1981 para 1.9

30 Melanie Henwood and Malcolm Wicks: *The Forgotten Army: family care and elderly people.* FPSC 1984

31 A Hunt: *The elderly at home* (1978) OPCS HMSO

32 The Audit Commission (1985) *Managing Social Services for the Elderly More Effectively* HMSO

33 Peter Townsend: *Poverty in the United Kingdom.* Penguin, 1979

34 Parker 1985 op cit

35 Ibid p13

36 Ibid

37 Equal Opportunities Commission, *Caring for the Elderly and Handicapped: community care policies and women's lives.* EOC 1982, p8

38 Henwood and Wicks, 1984 op cit

39 A Hunt: *A Survey of Women's Employment* 1986, HMSO

40 A Hunt 1978, op cit

41 Martin and Roberts, 1984, op cit, p114

42
The Experience of Caring for Elderly and Handicapped Dependents, Equal Opportunities Commission, 1980

43 Parker, 1985, op cit, p31

44 M Nissel and L Bonnerjea: *Family care of the handicapped elderly: who pays?* PSI 1982

45 Ibid p41

46 Ibid p66

47 R Jowell & C Airey (eds): *British Social Attitudes:* The 1984 Report. Gower, 1984, p95

48 Ibid

49 E Wilson: "Women, the 'community' and 'family' in A Walker (ed), *Community Care, the Family, the State and Social Policy*, 1982, Basil Blackwell

50 H Graham 'Women's poverty and caring' in C Glendinning and J Millar (eds) *Women and Poverty in Britain*, Wheatsheaf, 1987 p223

51 Ibid

52 Nissel & Bonnerjea, 1982, op cit

53 Ibid, p23

54 P Moss, Community care and young children' in A Walker (ed) 1982, op cit, p134

55 Graeme Russell, 'Problems in role reversed families' in Lewis and O'Brien, 1987, op cit

56 Ibid, p165

Section 3 Paid Work

1 Ray Pahl: *Divisions of Labour*, Blackwell 1985, p63

2 *General Household Survey 1984*, OPCS HMSO 1986, Tables 6.1 and 6.3

3 Ibid, Table 6.5

4 P Moss: 'Parents at work' in P Moss and N Fonda (eds): *Work and the Family*, Temple Smith 1980

5 *General Household Survey 1984*, op cit. Table 6.7 shows a higher participation rate by married men with chkldren, compared to those without, but whereas 98% of married men with 2 dependent children were economically active, this was true of just 95% of these with four or more dependent children. Within this, the latter group have unemployment rates nearly three times higher than the former.

6 *General Household Survey 1982*, OPCS, HMSO 1984, Table 6.23 and *General Household Survey 1984*, op cit, Tables 6.18 and 6.20

7 J Martin and C Roberts: *Women and Employment*, DE/OPCS HMSO, 1984 p98

8 *GHS* 1984, op cit, Table 6.17

9 Martin & Roberts, 1984, op cit, p98

10 Ibid

11 Young & Willmott, 1973, op cit p122

12 Martin and Roberts, 1984, op cit, table 4.11

13 Martin & Roberts, 1984, op cit, Table 9.5

14 Martin and Roberts, 1984, op cit, p130

15 Martin and Roberts, 1984, op cit, Table 9.15

16 S Moylan, J Millar, R Davies, *For Richer or Poorer*, DHSS cohort study of men entering unemployment in 1978. DHSS, Social Research Branch, Research Report No 11, HMSO 1984

17 C Smee and J Stern *The unemployed in a period of high unemployment*, Government Economic Service Working Paper No 11, HMSO 1978, p10

18 Martin and Roberts, 1984, op cit, Table 8.3

19 S Moylan & R Davies: 'The flexibility of the unemployed', DEG January 1981

20 K Cooke: 'Labour Supply behaviour of wives of the unemployed', Social Policy Research Unit, University of York 1985

21 K Cooke: 'Incomes in and out of work: a longitudinal analysis of the FFS and FRS'. Paper for the ESRC Social Security Research Workshop, February 1984

22 *Women's participation in paid work: Further analysis of the women and employment survey*, Department of Employment Research Paper No 45, 1984

23 A Hunt, *A Survey of Women's Employment*, HMSO 1968, p185, quoted in A Marsh, *Women and Shiftwork*, OPCS/HMSO, 1979, p81

24 Ibid, p81

25 Martin & Roberts, 1984, op cit, p171

26 Martin & Roberts, 1984, op cit, p107

27 Martin & Roberts, 1984, op cit, p177

28 R Jowell & S Witherspoon (eds) *British Social Attitudes, the 1985 Report*, Gower 1985, Ch 3

Section 4 Income and Resources

1 Barbara Wootton (1967). *In a world I never made*. Autobiographical Reflections, p159. George Allen & Unwin

2 Law Commission, *Transfer of Money between Spouses*. Law Commission Working Paper, No 90, HMSO 1985

3 A Marsh, *Women and Shift work*, OPCS. HMSO, 1979, pp11 and 12

4 Martin & Roberts, 1984, op cit, p99

5 Gail Wilson, 'Money: Patterns of responsibility and irresponsibility in marriage' in J Brannen and G Wilson (eds) *Give and Take in Families*, Allen & Unwin 1987, p141

6 Hilary Graham, 'Being poor: perceptions and coping strategies of lone mothers' in Brannen and Wilson, 1987, op cit, p62

7 Jan Pahl, *Taxation and family financial management*. July 1985. Unpublished paper

8 Jan Pahl: 'Patterns of money management within marriage', *Journal of Social Policy* 1980, Vol 9 Part 3, pp313-335

9 Evans, J et al (1983) *Marriages and money: Forms of financial arrangement within the family*, mimeo, University of Surrey, Dept of Sociology

10 Quoted in H Land, Paper for the London Women's Liberation Campaign for legal and financial independence. Evidence for Report No 6, *Lower Incomes*, Royal Commission on the Distribution of Income and Wealth, HMSO 1978

11 A Marsh, 1979, op cit, p9

12 G Wilson, 1987, op cit

13 J Brannen and P Moss, 'Dual earner households: women's financial contributions after the birth of the first child', in Brannen and Wilson (eds) 1987, op cit

14 Lydia Morris and Sally Ruane, *Household finance management and labour market behaviour*, 1986. Report to the Department of Employment. Work and Employment Research Unit, Durham University, p35

15 Morris and Ruane, 1986, op cit, p47

16 Quoted by Pahl 1980, op cit

17 Morris & Ruane, 1986, op cit, p9

18 Meredith Edwards: *Financial Arrangements Within Families*. Research report for the National Women's Advisory Council, Canberra, 1981

19 Graham, 1987, op cit, p63

20 Ibid, p65

21 Jane Millar and Caroline Glendinning, 'Invisible Women, Invisible Poverty'. p13 in Glendinning and Millar (eds) *Women and Poverty in Britain*, Wheatsheaf, 1987

22 Nicola Charles and Marion Kerr, 'Just the way it is: Gender and age differences in family food consumption', in Brannen and Wilson (eds) 1987, op cit, p156

23 W W Daniel: *The PEP Survey on inflation*, PEP 1975

24 L Syson and M Young: 'Poverty in Bethnal Green' in M Young (ed) *Poverty Report 1974*, Temple Smith

25 Melanie Henwood and Malcolm Wicks, *Benefit or Burden? The objectives and impact of child support*. Family Policy Studies Centre, 1986.

26 A Walsh & R Lister, *Mother's Life Line: A survey of how much women use and value child benefit*, CPAG 1985

27 A Cragg and T Dawson: *Unemployed women: A study of attitudes and experiences*. Research Paper No 47, Department of Employment

28 Cragg and Dawson, op cit, p52

29 Ibid, p53

30 Morris & Ruane, 1986, op cit, pp45-46

31 Ibid

32 Morris & Ruane, 1986, op cit, p107

33 Ibid

34 R Lister, *As Man and Wife: A Study of the Cohabitation Rule*, CPAG 1973. Poverty research series No 2

35 A new survey on financial arrangements after divorce is being conducted by OPCS.

Section Five   Private Families and Public Policy

1 Quoted in D Fraser, *The Evolution of the British Welfare State*, Macmillan 1973, p155

2 *Social Insurance and Allied Services*, Report by Sir William Beveridge, 1942, Cmnd 6404, para 108

3 Op cit, para 339

4 J MacNicol, *The Movement for Family Allowances 1918-45*, 1980, Heinemann, p28

5 See F Field, *Poverty and Politics*. The inside story of the CPAG campaigns in the 1970s, 1982, Heinemann

6 Lesley Rimmer, *The Changing Family:* the unit of assessment in the tax and benefits systems, National Consumer Council, 1984, p2

7 Ibid, p2

8 *The Taxation of Husband and Wife*, 1980, Cmnd 8093; *The Reform of Personal Taxation*, 1986, Cmnd 9756

9 Lesley Rimmer, op cit, p3

10 Melanie Henwood & Malcolm Wicks *Forgotten Army: family care and elderly people*, Briefing Paper 1984, FPSC

11 Explanatory memorandum to the 1983 Matrimonial and Family Proceedings Bill